The Early Years Curriculum: a view from outdoors

The Early Years Curriculum: a view from outdoors

Gloria Callaway

David Fulton Publishers

David Fulton Publishers Ltd
The Chiswick Centre, 414 Chiswick High Road, London W4 5TF

www.fultonpublishers.co.uk

First published in Great Britain by David Fulton Publishers in 2005

10 9 8 7 6 5 4 3 2 1

David Fulton Publishers is a division of Granada Learning Limited, part of ITV plc.

British Library Cataloguing in Publication Data
A catalogue record for this book is available from the British Library.

ISBN 1-84312-345-2

Typeset by FiSH Books, London
Printed and bound in Great Britain

Contents

Preface

Kernow Woodland Learning is based on the principles and practice outlined in the National Curriculum Guidance for the Foundation Stage. It began at Camborne Nursery School, Cornwall, as a pilot project to teach small groups of pupils outdoors in the woodlands for one session a week. With funding from the Camborne Pool Redruth Success Zone, it has now expanded to include most schools in the zone.

Significant events we remember from our own early education happened almost invariably when we were engaged in something practical, creative, challenging and successful. Such events happen weekly for these children.

This record aims to capture the delight, pleasure and sheer joy of everyone taking part, to celebrate the considerable achievements of all the children and adults involved.

The book aims to inform and inspire, to show how this model of learning complements and extends school-based education, and argues that it should be a basic entitlement for all children.

The educational principles, management and organisation of the project are outlined for colleagues wishing to undertake similar work. Examples and analysis of excellent teaching and learning strategies are described, as models for any of us wishing to improve our own practice. The book charts children's learning through purposeful play, using first-hand experience as the starting point for conceptual development, increased confidence and independence.

Like much of Cornwall, the Camborne Pool Redruth area has significant unemployment and other challenges more readily associated with inner-city districts. Beyond the beautiful beaches, harbours, gardens and cliffs of which Cornwall is so proud, there is widespread poverty and deprivation. The families of many children taking part in this project need considerable support, which was an important factor in the decision of local schools to bid for 'Education Action Zone' status.

Kernow Woodland Learning

The writer researched and documented the project over three years, through regular visits, discussions with colleagues, documentary and video evidence. The account offered is an accurate one, by a fellow practitioner who recognises and appreciates good practice in action; there was no need for 'biased' editing, rather a problem of not being able to share with readers even more details of the excellent work.

Leaders in all sessions described were women, because, to date, there is no fully qualified male 'advanced leader', although several men are working towards this. Men have been fully involved since the outset of the project, but early years education is, after all, an area where women are in the majority. Pronouns are accurate; there is no 'positive' or 'negative' discrimination.

Thank you!

- to the children, who were kind enough to accept and tolerate the strange person who joined them in the woodland to do her writing!

- to all the schools, for their enthusiasm and their faith in KWL.;

- to all the adults involved, who work so hard in the woodland and at school to further the aims of the project;

- to colleagues who have taken the time to read and provide feedback for this book;

- to Alan Worth and Nina Stibbe of David Fulton Publishers, for making it happen;

- to everyone who contributed data and photographs, especially Mark Holmes and his camera;

- to Andy Barclay and his colleagues at Cornwall Outdoor Education, for invaluable contributions to setting up the original project, and for on-going inputs into KWL training sessions;

- to Tony Sciascia, Tehidy Countryside Ranger, for his continuing support and assistance;

- to Julia Bond, who has advised and supported the project from the outset;

- to Judith Bower, who was instrumental in devising, designing and implementing the pilot project;

- to Paul Hanbury, Director of CPRSZ, and his team, for their goodwill and encouragement;

- most especially to Sandie Hawkey, KWL Project Leader, for her excellent work, unfailing good humour, energy and leadership;

- above all, to Jean Webb, whose vision, expertise and dedication provided the driving force for the project, and whose support and contributions were invaluable in the production of this book.

For further information, contact Sandie Hawkey,
Kernow Woodland Learning Project Leader
01209 610746
email shawkey@learningspace.co.uk

Photographs alongside accounts of particular sessions were not necessarily taken at the same time. Most have been contributed to the project by practitioners, too numerous to mention individually.

Introduction to Kernow Woodland Learning

Camborne Pool Redruth Success Zone, in the heart of Cornwall's once thriving mining district, hosts and funds Kernow Woodland Learning. Children go to the woods weekly to work with a qualified leader. The introduction traces the project's background, and outlines its principles.

Introduction

Kernow Woodland Learning acknowledges and appreciates the inspiration and initial impetus of the Bridgwater Forest School, itself based on a Danish model, which has generated considerable interest throughout the UK and western Europe. A visit to Denmark in the 1980s by Nursery Nurse students at Bridgwater College inspired the establishment of one on similar lines, funded by Bridgwater Education Action Zone.

Jean Webb, then Headteacher at Camborne Nursery School, Judith Bower, then in Cornwall's Early Years Education Team, Sandie Hawkey, then Teaching Assistant at Camborne Nursery School, and Andy Barclay, then with Cornwall Outdoor Education, visited Bridgwater. A pilot project was set up at the nursery school, to run through the spring and summer terms.

The location was chosen after a great deal of research at nearby Tehidy, where extensive woodlands are a reasonable driving distance from the school. Near the local golf course, it is easily accessible, and managed by Tehidy Countryside Rangers, who have been closely involved from the outset.

Consideration was given to access and parking, security, variety of plant life, health and safety, and the potential for setting appropriate boundaries. With some modifications, the site was ideal.

The project's aims were:

- to provide opportunities for the children to experience the outdoors, for half a day a week over a ten-week period;
- to encourage children to respect the outdoors: diverse weather conditions, the beauty and forms of nature and the changing seasons;
- to provide opportunities to develop a sense of awe and wonder;
- to complement and extend the indoor curriculum;
- to track children's development and achievement, with particular emphasis on speaking and listening, and social and emotional development.

The woodland is the 'classroom', and the clearing chosen for the 'base camp' is close to the road. It is reached via a path cut through the undergrowth with the co-operation of the countryside rangers, joining several existing trails. In base camp, logs arranged in a loose circle provide seating and an assembly point, with shelter provided, if really necessary, by a tarpaulin strung between the trees.

All planning was based on the Foundation Stage Curriculum's six areas of learning:

Personal, Social and Emotional Development   *Communication, Language and Literacy*
Mathematical Development   *Knowledge and Understanding of the World*
Creative Development   *Physical Development*

The current model stems from this work, which has been enhanced following rigorous evaluation. To date, almost every school in the zone with young children has taken advantage of the scheme, which has promoted considerable staff development as well as children's learning. Initially, this project was also called 'Forest School', but the time came to re-name it, to reflect:

- its location: **KERNOW** is Cornish for Cornwall;
- the **WOODLAND** environment in which it operates – there are no forests in Cornwall;
- the emphasis on **LEARNING** in, through and about the outdoors.

During their visits, children cover all areas of the curriculum, learning through purposeful play which relates directly to the woodland environment.

They tackle fun challenges at their own levels of competence; think creatively to solve problems; extend their reasoning, observational and creative powers, and develop their mathematical, scientific, language, social and physical skills.

They gain knowledge and understanding, confidence and self-esteem, as they take responsibility for themselves and each other, under the watchful eye of the adults. They have time to think, to play, to absorb the sights and sounds of the woodland, time to discover some of its treasures, and time to stand and stare.

Over the weeks, they see the natural world changing: leaves grow, become brittle on the branches and die; fungi sprout up and disappear; ferns gradually unfurl and flowers change colour.

KWL is set in an education action zone, which is, by definition, an area where children and their families need more support than most. However, this model was not planned specifically to meet the needs of children with learning, maturational, physical or behavioural difficulties, although pupils with these special needs have certainly benefitted. During the pilot, Jean Webb was very concerned to monitor its impact on a diverse group of children with very specific developmental needs. She felt strongly that if the work was of particular benefit to these children, it would surely function as a developmental support for the needs of all children.

One child, highly capable in pen and paper activities, was failing to engage in early writing and reading, despite her obvious potential, for fear of being 'wrong'. Jean wanted to develop her ability to take risks, and to work with others. In the woods, the child learned confidence in climbing and jumping, and was able to negotiate and co-operate with her peers when working on imaginative sculptures as a group activity. Close monitoring indicated that all the children made significant, even remarkable, progress in their areas of need during and after the project. In each case, this was directly attributed, by families and school staff, to their experiences in the woodland.

The concern to take full account of children's dispositions and attitudes to learning, making provision for investigating, hypothesising and taking risks, informed and inspired the entire project. During the evaluation, it became clear that such challenging and successful learning would be beneficial to all children, including, but not exclusively for, those with special needs.

This is no 'added extra', not just a 'treat', more than 'nature study' or a 'mini outward bound'; it is an integral element of the curriculum, which develops from week to week. One-off visits have an important place in education, but this is a continuing, evolving experience. This book unashamedly attempts to offer the evidence that KWL works, because those involved know it does.

The weekly routine

Each week, there is a regular pattern of events, to which the children soon become accustomed. Within this predictability, there is always something new and exciting to see, do and make. The routine is outlined below, with more detailed accounts of particular activities in following chapters.

Getting there

The minibus comes to take the children and adults to the woods. Children are already changed into appropriate outdoor clothes, and eager to get going to see what's the same and what's new in the woods this week. While getting dressed, they discuss concepts like 'weatherproof' and 'waterproof', and which fabrics are best for today's temperature and conditions. At school, at 'playtime', they can go inside if the weather takes a turn for the worse, so the discussion has a real purpose, because they will stay outdoors even if it rains.

On the bus, there is a seat belt ceremony; they know they must be properly strapped in, and each belt is checked before they set off. During the trip, children and adults recall what happened last week, and anticipate what lies ahead today in the woods.

They note familiar landmarks, making active use of mathematical terms to do with time and distance, like 'early', 'late', and 'nearly there'. The journeys there and back are integral to the experience, so this is more than an ordinary bus ride.

At Tehidy, the KWL leader is waiting for them as they manage the big step down from the bus. She greets them by name after the first time, and they spend a few minutes thinking about what they need to look out for. In effect, the children do their own 'risk assessment', before setting out on the trail through the trees to base camp. They know where to go, because blue string is tied at regular intervals along the path to mark the way.

Walking through the woodland

One advantage of being in well-established woodland is the very fact that it is somewhat hazardous. Most children live and play in comparatively sanitised, risk-free environments, with pavements designed precisely to minimise risk of tripping or stumbling. Here, children learn to walk safely on damp paths, to look out for obstacles, and whether it is sensible to touch something they find. Berries and fungi are beguiling things, but children soon learn that they are to look at, not to touch. There are lots of things they can touch, so this embargo does not seem like a big constraint, but a rather exciting taste of danger.

Health and safety is a way of working, regularly reinforced through games and discussions. Explanations are to do with 'why' rather than 'why not', and children are taught the reasons for the conventions they must follow.

Assumptions that there are regular tumbles and falls in the woods are wrong, even after heavy rain fills hollows in the ground, and paths are potential skid-tracks. Children are taught to recognise and deal with roots, slippery leaves and uneven paths, so accidental falls are rare. It is not a problem if someone trips, or a bramble attaches itself to a coat. An adult is nearby to talk over such incidents, so children's knowledge and understanding of the woods increases, as does their respect for it.

The walk can be quite brisk, or more leisurely, depending on what there is to examine on the way, but it is always relaxed. The leader already knows what might catch their eye, because she has walked the path to do a safety check beforehand. Her records from the previous session also help her to key in to what might interest this particular group today.

The influences of the changing seasons on light, temperatures, colours, flora and fauna, are part of planning, but spontaneous responses to such a rich and varied setting are equally important. Being in the woodland is special, with all its history evident in the mature trees, bushes, ground cover plants and creatures. There is always time to examine colours, forms, textures, smells and sounds. Children are encouraged to look up, down and around, to appreciate the 'big picture' of enormous trees, swathes of bluebells and tangled creepers, as well as the minute details of leaves, berries, insects, fungi and other fascinating woodland features. The focus tends to be botanical, but every opportunity is taken to explore mini-beasts, mammals and birds, and their interrelationships.

Base camp; hide and seek

When they see a tree with a splendid orange tie, they know they are near base camp, with logs to sit on and occasionally, if it is raining or likely to rain, a tarpaulin to provide a little shelter. Four trees with ties mark the boundaries to the north, south, east and west, beyond which children must have an adult in tow. Inside base camp, they are free to move around, being always in sight of an adult.

Once they have settled, with coats tucked in if the logs are wet, because there are no cushions, they play hide and seek, to remind them of base camp rules, and to reacquaint them with the area. Children choose a hiding place, and the adult goes too. Hiding in groups gives them a strategy in the unlikely event that they lose sight of the rest of the group. They also get very proficient at counting to twenty as the weeks go by.

Everyone has a turn at hiding and seeking, including the adults, who enjoy it as much as the children. Then, there is time to talk about what happened last week, to recap on this week's walk and what was the same and what was different.

The first challenge

The leader introduces the first task or activity, with a story, a demonstration or a suggestion, based on one or more areas of learning.

The children discuss how they might carry out the task. They are reminded of what is and is not possible, and care is taken to make sure adults and children are quite clear about the expectations.

One activity involves children collecting five items of a particular colour. First, the leader checks if they understand 'five' and know the colour, and that there are enough items to have five each. Collecting 'five' becomes more complex on a later visit; they are each asked to collect five yellow, five green and five brown leaves, to sort from the oldest to the newest. This needs mathematical and scientific skills as well as colour recognition, so it provides excellent teaching opportunities.

By the time they go to explore, everyone knows what to do, and how to begin, confident that they can accomplish the task. They use twigs, sticks, leaves and other woodland resources to make shelters for badgers, patterns in the environment, 'smell pots', weavings, sculptures and furniture. They watch a fire being lit, and learn the difference between smoke from the fire and steam from the water which douses it. They collect beaters to make music, and listen to the different sounds. They use all their senses, except taste, because eating things found in the woods is not a good idea.

They might work in small groups with an adult, or individually. The leader may take a group herself, but more often she visits each group in turn to see their decision-making processes in action. Sometimes, everyone works together. There is variety, and scope to try out different ways of working.

The weather influences activities; rushing around on hot days is not a good idea, even in the shade. In the cold, they need more physical activity, depending on how slippery the ground is. The tarpaulin can inspire exciting investigations, especially when rain lies on it in heavy puddles, or leaf silhouette shadows are visible above.

The meticulous planning which went into devising these tasks and challenges may not be immediately obvious to a casual observer of young children doing fun things in the woods. It all seems very straightforward, as it should, but the efforts of a highly expert early years team should not be taken for granted, nor should the skills required to make it work.

Tasks and activities are designed to be:

- clear and simple, giving children confidence that they can attempt them without stress;
- appropriate for children's levels of confidence and understanding;
- challenging, to encourage new thinking, without being frustrating for the group;
- achievable within a specified time, using available materials;
- open-ended, with an infinite number of ways to complete; there is no predetermined product for the children to copy or match.

They are framed to encourage children to make informed guesses, anticipate, estimate, reason and fathom things out for themselves.

If they have a problem, an adult can help them think it through. The advantage of careful, learning-based plans is that adults can focus on these as they assess the children's actions and words, and give appropriate support and assistance.

If the first activity has been to make or find things, the results are shown off and admired by all. This is an opportunity for the adults to compliment the children on what they have done, and to point out what they have learned. The pride in their own and others' achievements is a delight for all. That children learn without noticing may be true, but it is important to acknowledge what they have learned. Mathematical understanding is shown in estimating, measuring, counting, or making sets of like items. Scientific understanding is demonstrated in working out if tracks were made by a bird or a mammal. Praise is given to budding mathematicians, scientists, gymnasts and problem-solvers alike.

Hot chocolate and biscuits

Everyone sits on logs, anticipating the hot chocolate drink and biscuit that they know will follow their exertions. The leader makes the drink with hot water from a flask, following the children's instructions quite often, because sometimes she forgets, or tries to do things in the wrong order. But they remember the sequence after the first time, motivated by the reward of the drink at the end of the process.

They count cups, hand out biscuits, and make sure that everyone is included. How many children? How many adults? How many altogether? Will the robin come by as usual to see if there are crumbs to spare? What shall we do next?

This is also a time to relax, to mull over the events of the session so far, and to listen to the sounds of the woodland.

Snack time is unpredictable in some ways, because it can be time for uproarious laughter and giggling, led by the children, about a bizarre idea or word-play, but it can equally be a time for quiet contemplation and concentration. Once the cups have been counted back in, and the flask put away, there is time built in for free play within base camp, before the next activity.

The second challenge

Some activities involve strenuous effort and physical skill, like tree-climbing, mud-sliding, making log trails and rope-swinging. Children operate within their own personal limits, but are encouraged to stretch those limits, to develop judgement and physical skills, and to be adventurous while taking responsibility for their own safety. Adults talk children through these activities, but never physically lift a child beyond where she or he can safely reach alone.

Hoisting a child to a high branch, or catching a child who jumps, is not a bad thing in itself, but the emphasis here is on personal responsibility for personal decisions. Lifting takes away their personal control, and sends the message: *You can't do this on your own*, rather than: *I'll help you to do this by yourself*. With help, children gradually develop skills of balance, learn how to use hands and feet to support their body weight, use hand–eye and hand–foot co-ordination, and gain confidence.

Time to go

Whatever the activity, the base camp part of the session ends with everyone seated to reflect briefly on the events of the day. There are thank yous, and reminders of what has been achieved, and everyone is usually amazed at just how much has been done in just one and a half to two hours.

They check the time to see how long it will be before the bus comes, because this influences the pace of the walk from base camp back to the road. They may take their time, or have to rush.

Weary children and adults climb aboard the bus to go back to school. They may be clutching things they have collected, and they may have muddy clothes and shoes. What they certainly take back to school with them is the experience and, usually, the happy expectation that they will return next week at the same time for more fun.

Sessions follow a set pattern, because routines are so important for young children. Being in the woods for several consecutive weeks means there is time to establish and repeat the routine, so the group can relax, absorb the atmosphere and be comfortable. These are preconditions for young children's effective learning, and the exciting challenges are all the more attainable because of the ambience in which they are set. Timings vary considerably, but the overall routine is:

Getting ready:
- choosing clothes, putting them on;
- working out when the bus will come;
- saying goodbye to friends at school;
- greeting the bus and driver;
- getting on the bus, checking seat belts.

Getting there:
- the bus journey, the landmarks;
- how long it takes, how far it is;
- undoing seat belts, climbing down;
- meeting and greeting the leader;
- recapping what to look for in the woods.

Walking the blue string trail:
- following a familiar path, noting what has changed since last time;
- looking out for hazards;
- talking about what is around them;
- stopping to share observations with the rest of the group.

Arriving at base camp:
- settling down on the log seats;
- remembering and rehearsing the names of the boundary trees;
- playing hide and seek;
- remembering what they did last time, and anticipating what they will do today.

The first challenge:
- listening to the brief for the first activity;
- discussing alternative ways of achieving it;
- making groups and working on the challenge;
- discussing how to get it right;
- deciding when it is finished;
- sharing everyone's work.

Snack time:
- making and drinking hot chocolate;
- handing out and eating the biscuits;
- relaxing and conversing;
- clearing up cups and chocolate making kit;
- playing freely in base camp;
- assembling again to see what's next.

The second challenge:
● listening, talking;
● doing, sharing;
● talking about what happened.

Getting ready to go:
● tidying up;
● picking up belongings;
● walking back to the bus;
● thank yous and goodbyes.

The journey back:
● getting on the bus;
● talking about the day;
● having a rest;
● anticipating what to tell everyone at school.

Each element is equally important, contributing to children's developing understanding in all the areas of learning. What happens back at school, and at home, is also highly significant as children talk about their experiences and use them as the basis for further activities.

Base camp is left clean and tidy, and the tarpaulin is removed, if it is not needed again that day.

The next section looks in more detail at how particular groups have tackled particular challenges, and analyses the teaching and learning opportunities afforded by the experience.

Principles into practice

Through accounts of typical sessions, this section examines how children learn while they walk through the woods; make base camp; name the trees; play hide and seek; enjoy snack time; make environmental art; make sounds in the woodland; and toast marshmallows on a fire. It also considers follow-up activities back at school.

The blue string trail

The minibus parked on the main path and its occupants disembarked to meet the leader. This is the starting point for their weekly walk through the couple of hundred yards to base camp, but this is much more than an access route. Blue string, tied at regular intervals on branches, indicates the way. Children learn that, each time they reach a marker, they should look for the next.

Then, they can proceed with confidence, concentrating on what they see and hear, touch and smell.

On this occasion, the leader spotted some spectacular fungi on the path, just beyond where the bus stops. She showed the children, and teased back the leaves around the two large yellow forms, because everyone knows you do not touch.

Children love the words 'fungus' and 'fungi'. They know what they look like, and can use the words accurately, but had not realised that each fungus has its own name.

The leader had consulted her reference book earlier, and got it out to show the children. Pages were turned until they reached pictures of similarly coloured fungi. They scrutinised them, and found one that looked like theirs. They all agreed that 'buttercap' was a very good name.

This incidental use of a reference text demonstrates how to satisfy your curiosity, if you happen to have the right book. Non-fiction texts are often underused with young children, but even 'grown-up' books can be accessible with a little help. They had learned a lovely new word, but, even more importantly, they had been motivated to learn how to find what they wanted from the book.

At the start of the blue string trail, there was a short recap on the risks to look out for on the way. Children led the discussion, effectively carrying out a risk assessment for themselves.

What do we think about when we walk through the woods?
Roots. You've got to step over them.

Can we see one?
Yes – there – and there!

The roots were examined; the leader wondered where they came from. The children took the cue, following the root across the path, to see which tree it belonged to. Later, they might trace more roots, and perhaps find out which sort of tree has the biggest ones. They might look at photographs of trees and roots back at school. Next week, they might think about how some roots are very near the surface, while others go deep underground.

A distraction arrived, in the shape of a familiar small brown bird with a distinctive red breast, which often appears just here, as does another at base camp.

Why do we think the robin follows us on the path?
A pause; everyone had always taken it for granted.
What's on the ground just here?
Leaves. And mud – we get mud all over our boots!
And, when we walk along, what happens to the leaves?
They get all kicked up.
I wonder what lives under the leaves?
Insects. Is the robin after the insects to eat?

Gently prompted to make connections and deductions, they have come to a further understanding of the relationship between the robin and themselves, and perhaps learned that there might just be an ulterior motive to the bird's apparent friendship.

Back at school, there are books and other resources to glean more information about this bird, its territorial and nesting habits, and its camouflage.

Reference books are useful for children and adults, because few of us know as much as we might about even the most familiar creatures and plants. Without knowing how, where and when a robin builds a nest, how many eggs are in a clutch, how long they live, and what other birds share the territory, we cannot ask the right questions to encourage the children to make deductions. Saying, 'how interesting!' is not enough, so subject knowledge is vital, even if we are not experts.

A little further on, a child stopped to examine strange round-ish objects on the path. They have been seen before, but this week the leader probed a little further on the subject of oak galls.

I wonder what it is?
It looks like a slug. It's all slugged up.
It's like a ball shape.
The leader explained about the insect inside. They all looked.
Can you see it? Look! I can.
I think they're sleeping.

In the last stretch before base camp, children went to look at the ferns, which had delighted them by gradually uncurling week by week. There were some brown ones alongside fresh green ones, which promoted a short discussion about whether they were alive or dead. The children noticed other differences too, which could lead to a focus on closer identification of fern varieties on a future occasion.

In less than twenty minutes since they arrived, this group of children had:

- learned that fungi have distinct varieties and names, which can be looked up in a book;
- traced the inconvenient root back to its tree;
- found out about the insect 'all slugged up' inside the oak gall, so named because only oak trees have them;
- realised that robins like to eat insects from under leaves without having to dig, if they can, and
- worked out that ferns wither and die, but not necessarily all at the same time.

Base camp

Base camp is at the heart of the whole experience, not a sophisticated 'den', but a series of logs enclosing part of a small clearing, bounded by tall deciduous trees and bushes. Each group arranges the logs on their first visit, with technical tips from the adults. From then on, it is their meeting place and the focus for group discussions. Organising base camp helps the children to 'make their mark' on their new surroundings: it also gives them a good reason to explore the area, because there is a practical problem to solve.

What can we sit on?
We could sit on the leaves.
Some did, but it was uncomfortable.
What if it rains? We'll get wet bottoms!
J made a cushion of dry ferns.
Oh! That will be prickly!

They considered different solutions, trying to find seats which were likely to be dry, smooth and comfortable, not prickly, not scratchy. One of the children spotted a log a few yards away. This clearly had potential, but there was still a series of challenging problems to solve. Adults had already worked out a solution for this problem, but the children needed to find their own way to do it.

How can we get it over here?
We can push with our feet.
They soon found out that it is a bit hard for small feet to push such a big log.
What else could we use?
Hands!
OK. The leader demonstrated how to push it.
We need to make sure there is no-one on that side. Why?
It will roll over them!

Yes, so we need to be sure to do it safely.
The leader and two of the children rolled the log into the clearing.
Is it big enough for all of us?
They tried it out, squashing themselves uncomfortably on the log.
It's too short! We need some more.

They went to look. N found one, then another, then another. In turn, they were moved into the base camp area, placed randomly in the space. The children sat, but they could not all see each other, so another arrangement was needed.

We can put them like that!
N demonstrated rows, and the logs were moved again, as she had suggested.

The children learned, through trial and error, that equal pressure or force needed to be applied at either end to move the logs forwards, or more on one side than the other to move them at an angle. The force had to be consistent if the logs were to move as and where they needed them. Laughter seemed to help them move better too.

Once the desired arrangement had been achieved, it was assessed. Everyone sat, in rows, facing the same way, and still could not all see and hear each other.

We can make a circle!
We sit in a circle in school.
We can see each other in school!

By now, the children were very good at log-moving, so they quickly rearranged the logs into a more circle-like shape. This worked better on the whole, and became the arrangement for future sessions. They tested the logs' stability, rolling them gently with their feet, and they were a bit wobbly. So they decided it was best to step over them, not on top.

The principle of hypothesising, testing and evaluating different plans may sound a little overblown for eight small children moving some logs, but this is exactly what they were encouraged to do.

Once evaluated, a plan can be adapted or adopted. No suggestion was 'wrong', but they had the opportunity to work towards the most satisfactory solution in their own way, in their own time.

Now, all voices could be heard, no matter how shy and muted. In this 'democratic' layout, body language and eye contact can encourage responses and suggestions. It can also facilitate silent interactions, non-verbal shared moments which can be very precious.

In base camp, children listen carefully, because information and tasks are important; there is good reason to concentrate. Comments are rarely 'off task', because children are interested. Inappropriate remarks or behaviour are treated positively but firmly. This increases children's self-esteem: they are motivated to behave well, so they do. They do not get told off, so they feel good. This is intrinsic motivation – 'good' behaviour for its own sake. In any case, there are no stickers or stars on offer.

By managing and arranging this space, children have an investment, an ownership; it is theirs to enjoy, and to be responsible for.

Naming the trees

Base camp is demarcated not by fences or barbed wire, but by four trees, each with a fluorescent orange ribbon tie. Children make friends with each tree in turn: they touch, look up at branches and down at roots, describe its features and talk about what it reminds them of. From these comments, a name emerges for each tree. Suggestions they make are combined into an original, descriptive name.

Chosen words indicate the range of concepts already familiar to the children, and their current preoccupations, like Bob the Builder. Children remember the names much better than adults. These are the delightful names given to each of the trees by twelve different groups.

The first tree

- Lumpy Tall Tree
- Bob the Builder Tree
- Bumpy Tree Wet
- Seaweed Bump Brush
- Four Point Huggy Tree
- Clickypickywicky Tree
- Hurt Prickly Tree
- Leaf Bumpy Tree
- Horsey Tie Tree
- Tall Tall Tree
- Spiky Grumpy Tree
- Warm Sunny Tree

The second tree

- Spiky Spongy Hand Tree
- Holly Daisy Tree
- Fallen Down Tree
- Bent Down Tree
- Soft Tree
- Boo Woo Campris Tree
- Peter Pan Tree
- Turn Around Bonfire Tree
- Soft Neaty Tree
- Cranky Tree
- Mr Wonky Tree
- Jungle Rope Tree

The third tree

- Bumpy Smooth High Tree
- Hot Chop Tree
- Wet Hard Tree
- Green Pen Tree
- Kelly Tree
- Long Mongy Tree
- Tickly Faraway Tree
- Tall Soft Smoothy Tree
- Carpet Tree
- Bumpy Tree
- Bumpy Lumpy Tree
- Hasty Green Fluffy Funny Tree

The fourth tree

- Hairy Tickly Tree
- Grassy Scratchy Twig Tree
- Stickyout Tree
- Grass Tree
- Bumpy Head Soft Tree
- Squeaky Tinkly Tree
- Tinker Blueberry Tree
- Big Tiny Short Tree
- Loggity Tree
- Spiky Tree
- Seaweednut Tree
- Rough Pricklybud Tree

Another group's naming ceremony went as follows. The leader could spy some special trees, different from the others. Children followed her eyes, and delightedly pointed to the orange-tied tree. Then, they noticed the others.

That one's got an orange ribbon too!
And that one! That one's got the same ribbon on!

The leader explained that base camp is inside these trees, and that they can play anywhere in this space. But they must not pass the orange ribbon trees without an adult. There was a small problem, though. How would everyone know which tree was which, when they all had the same ribbons? The children had no ideas, so the leader suggested that naming them might help. This was obviously a good idea.

Everyone stood by the first tree. J rubbed the nodules on the bark.
Oh – they feel hard.
Yes, she's right. They do feel a bit hard there.
Several people smoothed the lumps, and looked up at the enormous trunk.
The tree's growing sideways.
Yes – does that remind you of anything?
A slide.
Is that a good name for a tree? A slide?
It's a bumpy slide.
It's a bumpy slide tree!
And it's hard.

The tree was now officially *Hard Bumpy Slidey Tree.*

The model had been set: they could voice their ideas, which would be made into a name, which the leader would write down. They were ready to go to the next tree now, which H had spotted from the log seats. H took responsibility of leading the group to 'her' tree, and they all followed. She said nothing, relying on others to read her body language in order to communicate. They did, and she was fully included.

It's got something extra – look, what's that?
The children stroked the tree.
It's tickling hard.
What about that! L said it's a hard tickly tree. If you touch it just gently, especially this bit here, does it tickle your fingers?
Yes! It's tickly!

The leader's pen ran out, so the children promised to remember the name for her: *Hard Tickly Tree.*

N led the group to 'her' tree. There was a lovely hole in it.
You can see the ground – all the way round. All the way round to there!

The leader explained. Tony, the countryside ranger who looks after the woods, came to look and decided the tree was not safe. The children already knew why: there was a hole, and holes can make things break. Tony cut off the branch with his saw, because the hole in the middle made it weak.

And that had to be chop down because it's a crack!

K was clearly impressed. The leader wondered what to call it. A soft voice responded.

I know – it's spiky here!
The tree was named, Spiky Tree.

We leave them here to consider what learning has taken place during this activity. Some children may have had the opportunity to name a pet or a toy, but the power of being able to name a tree is palpable. Their words are given authenticity, status and longevity, through being recalled week after week, actively used by everyone in the group. Children are often asked to describe things, but naming the tree is significant because:

- it familiarises them with the extent of the base camp area;
- it helps them to remember the characteristics of a particular tree;
- it enables them to make connections between those qualities and their own previous experiences;
- it is a token of 'ownership';
- it encourages them to use all their senses, especially touch and sight.

The long, composite names are original and amusing. Most children enjoy getting to grips with multi-syllabic words, struggling to get the sounds in order, and committing them to memory; some readers will recall the complicated expression *supercalifragilisticexpialidocious* from *Mary Poppins*, which delighted a whole generation.

How clever these children are, to say *spikeyspongytree* or *roughpricklybudtree*, all in order, and to be understood by others. How proud they are, and rightly so.

This apparently simple activity typifies the quality of the pedagogical principles underpinning planning at KWL. Tree-naming is a great idea, but, more than that, it is based on a real understanding of how young children acquire concepts through first-hand experience, and how they learn that concepts can be applied beyond the initial exploration.

Names given to ideas and concepts such as 'spiky' and 'spongy' enable children to broaden their powers of expression. Names empower, because they help all of us to describe and articulate ideas which are otherwise hard to communicate.

Since this session was recorded, tree-naming has been modified, to ensure that each child makes a special relationship with one tree. First, children go in twos or threes, with an adult, to one tree and decide on a name, then visit the others to learn what their names are. In turn, children explain to each other why they called that tree that name, and the others practise and remember.

An analysis of the areas of learning covered in this activity is in Section Four.

One, two, three... Where are you?

The group reached base camp, and settled quickly on the logs. They rehearsed base camp rules, through playing a version of hide and seek, devised by the Bridgwater team. A small group of children hid in the woodland, beyond the boundary trees, accompanied by an adult. Others closed or covered their eyes, pulled down their hoods, or simply looked down at the ground while they counted to twenty, quite a challenge for some, to give the others time to hide.

After counting, the base camp group yelled: *One, two, three, where are you?* There was an echoing response: *One, two, three, we're here!* This was the signal to go and find them.

Which direction is the sound coming from?
Over there!
No, over there!
Over there!
They called again, to verify the direction.
One, two, three, where are you?
One, two, three, we're here!
Consensus reached, they ran to their friends.

This lively game fulfils a number of objectives beyond the fun and camaraderie it engenders. It sets a pattern, which the children can use if they suddenly feel insecure in the woodland. It reinforces boundaries, beyond which they must not go without an adult. It encourages them to listen intently, to work out directionality of sound, and they become more familiar with the area each time they play.

The small group hides together, with an adult; the rest seek together, with adults. So there must be general agreement for the game to work, and this sometimes needs time. It is part of the adults' role to balance the dynamics of the game with the need for children to understand agreement.

Once, a group was spotted very quickly, and children realised it was the adult's bright blue coat that gave away their hiding place. That led to a discussion of camouflage, and which colours stood out from the browns and greens of the woods.

'The best game ever' involved some very clever hiding, six calls and four or five minutes of seeking.

We didn't think you would ever find us!
You didn't see us – we're the same colour as the tree!

The group had not yet quite remembered the word 'camouflage', but demonstrated a firm grasp of the concept in action.

Snack time

About halfway through the session, the group assembled on the logs for snack time. Among her many duties, the leader ensures that hot water is available in a flask, along with a whisk, chocolate powder, mugs and biscuits. This particular snack time went like this.

The leader quietly got out the chocolate-making kit, but was nonetheless closely observed by all, as they cleaned their hands with wet wipes. The children knew the routine well, and always looked forward to the well-earned drink. They watched her put chocolate powder into a large jug, stirring it with the whisk. After a few seconds, she pronounced the chocolate made.

No – that's not how you do it!
You forgot the water!
She took a flask of cold water from her bag.
I'll pour it in.

No, no!
The children giggled, not believing this incompetence could really be true.
You've got to have the water from the flask!
You've got to have hot water to make chocolate!
Oh, yes. So I have.
The leader pressed the button on the large flask.
I wonder what that is, coming from the spout?
Water! Smoke! Steam!
It's steaming 'cos the weather's cold.
Oh, yes. Where else would you see steam?
Out the kettle.
On the barbecue.
Is the kettle steam or smoke?
Steam.
Is the barbecue steam or smoke?
Smoke, 'cos the coal's not wet.
And juice?
Juice is cold – it don't have steam. Nor smoke.

These four-year-olds were well on the way to having a firm grasp of an important scientific concept, and had used excellent recall and sequencing skills to direct the leader in her task.

Time for the cups. How many do we need?
The children counted. Today there were one – two – three adults.
But I'm four!

A classic confusion arose between number of adults and number of years. Who has had their fourth birthday? Who else is four years old? There were five four-year-olds, so this dilemma would not be sorted today, but the adult could reinforce the difference between ordinal and cardinal numbers back at school, or here next week.

Green cups are very popular. The children looked at the stack, and predicted who would be lucky today. The third one down was green, so who would get that one? The cups are always randomly stacked, so there is no favouritism. This can be hard for children who usually get exactly what they want at home, but they respect the 'rule', grin and bear it if their cup this week is yellow. F noticed that her cup changed colour as the brown liquid was poured in.

Look, it's a different colour down there!
Is it darker or lighter?
Don't know – it's browner.
Everyone's cup now had two colours.

This presented an opportunity to introduce the lovely word 'translucent'. The children had noticed how the light made the empty bit at the top of the cup glow, but the brown liquid showing through the bottom stopped the light from penetrating the plastic.

Eventually, they decided that the bottom was darker and the top was lighter: another discussion bearing on scientific understanding. Words like 'transparent' and 'opaque' might also creep into such a conversation. This is not just coincidence: it was one very good reason for choosing these cups.

Blowing the steam away helps hot drinks get cooler. The leader wondered why, but the children did not respond, so she did not press the point. They were busy working out whose biscuit had a cow on it, and which ones were best for dunking in hot chocolate. In the interests of scientific investigation, everyone had another biscuit that day, to compare and contrast their relative attributes. They had a special treat. The adults knew they were learning about scientific investigation. But the biscuits tasted just as good anyway!

Children absorbed in eating and drinking tend to be still, especially after energetic activity, so the sounds of the woodland have less competition. This is the time to hear the birds, the wind in the leaves, the imagined sounds of other woodland inhabitants and, sometimes, the rain on the tarpaulin.

Once everyone is refuelled, children help to collect the cups, and then they can play for a while in the immediate vicinity, before the next task.

Rearranging the woodland: environmental art

It is, with good reason, an oft-repeated cliché that all children are creative and imaginative. On the whole they are, but creativity involves the control of tools and materials, and the skills required to use them, to realise an idea or to make a product. So some teaching may be needed for it to develop appropriately. Children need to be given responsibility for creative decisions, without an adult imposing ideas about what it should look or sound like.

Children also need inspiration, and a clear starting point, so they can develop their skills and not be frustrated by being unable to do or make what they really want to achieve.

This task described below was inspired by the work of environmental artist Andy Goldsworthy, but these children used these woods, these current seasonal colours, and the available resources, to decorate a hole in the ground or a tree.

You can't decorate a hole!
You can decorate a tree – like Christmas!
We could have a paintbrush.
No – you don't use paintbrushes for trees!
There isn't any paintbrushes in the woods!
You could use leaves.

They discussed what sort of leaves might be good, and the children looked around and brought back some examples, to place on the ground for others to see.

Are all the leaves the same?
No – mine's crinkly, and that one isn't.
Mine's yellow!
Is mine a leaf?
Well, it's off a tree, but is it a leaf?
No – it's round and prickly. Leaves are flat.
It's from a chestnut tree, and it's the case the seed grows in.
We saw them on the path, when we walked to base camp. We saw them then.
We can use them, like stuff on a Christmas tree.

This was an important part of the activity, because children had a chance to try out ideas, and to hear other people's, before they began on their own decorative task.

They went in threes or fours with an adult, to look for a likely spot. Once they had selected the tree, or hole in the ground (because, after all, some people thought holes could be decorated), they scoured the immediate area for decorations. They knew that they should not pick anything living in the woods, so they used bits and pieces from the ground, or asked an adult if they were not sure.

How to attach one thing to another is a problem which design technologists, sculptors, engineers and needleworkers have to address. With no glue, string or sewing equipment, there had to be another way. If you just balanced something on the branch, it fell off, so that was no good. Some tried lengths of creeper to tie things together and found it worked, although it was a bit fiddly. Some decided to make holes in their decorations, and used the trees as spikes. This was quite effective on the holly tree, which had spikes galore, which they handled carefully so as not to get scratched.

It was easier for those working on the ground: they did not have gravity to contend with in the same way. If they put things on the ground, they stayed there.

They noticed some bluebell shoots which had grown right through the dead brown leaves on the ground. That was exactly what they had done on the tree! The new spiky shoots were not strong enough to dislodge the leaves, so they just grew through any hole they could find. How clever is a bluebell, and how clever of the children to notice, because none of the adults had.

They also noticed some small rocks on the ground which had not been evident before they started to work low down. There was time to have a good look at them, to discuss the colours and textures, before careful consideration of exactly where to place them in the arrangement around the hole.

The children eagerly showed an adult their discovery. She thought it might be granite, another new word today. It provided the final touch for the decoration, which was, the children now declared, finished. With a little time in hand, it was suggested that they might make a small trail, so the arrangement would be noticed from a distance. They knew exactly what they wanted to do.

Selecting materials, like a given number of leaves of a particular shape and colour, helps children learn to

classify, to choose and sort according to certain criteria. In rearranging items in new patterns, they make real mathematical and aesthetic judgements. If the pattern is regular, they need to estimate the distances between the items, and to decide which way round a leaf or twig should be. Some will opt for symmetry, and another new word will come into use.

Everyone went in turn to admire their friends' work, and to discuss how each group had met the same challenge in different ways. New ideas, words and discoveries about colours, materials and techniques they learned about today might be useful next time they do something similar.

Speaking to an audience is sometimes difficult, but when you have something you really want to say, that they really want to hear, it is much, much easier. So children are more articulate when they focus on what they want to talk about, and everyone else wants to hear.

Children understand, at a practical level, the idea that, if you change the position and arrangement of selected items, you enhance both the items and the place they are in. It is a regular seaside activity, and some of these children are familiar with the beach a couple of miles from home. It is an idea used by visual artists in many genres, especially environmental artists like Andy Goldsworthy.

It is totally inappropriate for children to copy artists' work, but here they are taking an idea and making it work for themselves, in their own space. They have photographs of artists' work at school, and they will understand it better because they have had a go themselves.

Examples of children's work demonstrate that negotiation, organisation, mathematical thinking, communication and co-operation happened during the process of making. The front cover portrays children who are very proud of the group effort in making a beautiful arrangement from leaves and sticks they have collected. It is this pride in a job well done, with effort and perseverance, which fosters self-esteem and a positive attitude to learning and life, and pleasure in the aesthetic products they have achieved.

A mathematical interlude

Meanwhile, back at one of the trees, a child had noticed a small branch sticking out at exactly the same height as him; when he stood under it, the branch just brushed the top of his head. He called everyone around to look, and they wondered if it would be the same for other children, or a bit too high, or a bit too low. Some had to stretch to reach the branch, and a couple nearly bent it, because they were too tall. But for three of them, it was just right. So, those three must be exactly the same height. They stood side by side, and they were. The tree measuring stick worked.

The mathematical concepts being rehearsed, consolidated and developed in this spontaneous activity were really quite exciting. The first child estimated that the branch was as high as he was tall; he tested this idea and found it was right. His friends also estimated: *I'm taller than him, so I won't fit*.

The children had demonstrated that they understood the concept of a measure. This is a highly significant feature of mathematical and scientific development. Making the leap of understanding that because two objects (in this case, bodies) fit exactly in the same place, those two objects must be the same size as each other, is an important and useful concept to acquire.

They also showed that they understood about estimating, making an informed guess about whether someone would or would not fit under the branch. This can be very disconcerting for children (and adults) who are concerned about getting things wrong.

Estimation is, essentially, a trial and error process. Anyone scared of making an error will avoid making an estimate, and so will be denied the experience of trying. Without informed guesses, most of us cannot function in daily life. Children making patterns and shapes in creative work also have to estimate if that might fit there, or if that will look too small over there. When building a shelter for the tallest person in the group, each stick is considered, and its length estimated, before deciding whether or not it will do the job. If it will, fine. If not, it has to be left where it is.

The many sounds of the woodland

Musical development involves listening to, and making, sounds. Gradually, there is an awareness of tempo, timbre, pitch, rhythm and texture in a range of musical genres. The ability to listen, and perhaps imitate and reproduce a sound, or a series of sounds, contributes greatly to children's understanding and appreciation of sounds and music. There are obvious links with the science of sound, as well as with pattern and aesthetic appreciation, visually and aurally.

In the woods, we can hear a range of sounds:

- **natural sounds**, like the wind in the leaves, rain on leaves and paths, birdsong;
- **'accidental' human sounds**, made just by being there, like walking on crunchy leaves or squelchy ground, brushing against foliage as they pass by;
- **deliberate human sounds**, their own and others' conversations, using their voices, or materials around them as instruments;
- **mechanical sounds**, like noises made by tractors, aeroplanes and the occasional helicopter.

Children can be helped to analyse and 'sort' the sounds into different types, especially during built-in quiet times, made for listening. They make sound together, using sticks to bang on logs, setting up rhythms for others to copy, following others' rhythms and taking turns to develop a series of sounds around the group. Percussive instruments are the most obvious sources of sounds, but wind instruments are also available, like voices, or blowing against a leaf or into a tree hollow. Such conscious, deliberate sound-making is the precursor to music-making; how far it develops into music is largely dependant on the skills of the leader. This account is of one group's exploration of sound.

The leader suggested they close their eyes and listen. They knew all about listening, because they had practised it playing hide and seek, so they shut their eyes, screwed up their faces to show how much they were concentrating, and listened.

I heard a car!
Ssh! We have to listen!

The others were not yet ready to break the comparative quiet, so he stopped talking. This was quite a step for him, because he was not known for his powers of concentration, nor for his willingness to take notice of others' concerns. After a while, each child quickly named something he or she heard, and the others listened for it too.

Everyone was asked to step back over the logs, then to sit or kneel facing inwards.

The leader beat the log in front of her with the palms of both hands, and asked them to do it too. A demonstration of how to keep fingers extended and hands stretched showed them how, and they copied her. Once it was clear that everyone had managed this, she began a basic, repetitive, steady rhythm, and they all joined in.

The sound got softer, and she asked them if they could make soft, quiet sounds too, and they could.

The rhythm stayed the same, as they focused on the volume. When they could cope with this, the rhythm was varied, to slow, slower, faster, very fast. There was total concentration.

When the leader paused, so did they, putting hands in laps just like her. One child was invited to tell the others what sort of sound he would like them to make. *Can you make a noisy sound?* He demonstrated. The others copied, and in turn each had a chance to ask everyone to make loud, quiet, soft, slow, fast, noisy sounds.

Children listened to each other, giving and taking instructions, following or taking the lead, each making a small contribution to a group effort.

The leader was keen to stretch their powers of concentration as far as possible. The first time in the woods, they were more restless, eager to explore a new space, but now they could focus for longer.

The leader beat the log with a stick.
Could you make a sound like that?
Her eyes signalled that, if they looked down, they might find sticks. They did, and beat the logs just as she had, with energy. The leader asked J and W to make sounds in turn, so the others could hear.
Does J's stick sound the same as W's?
No.
Why not?
'Cos my one's fat and big, and his one is little and thin!

In that short sentence, we hear scientific understanding: big fat sticks sound different from little thin sticks; use of the descriptive words we call adjectives; and an indication of mathematical appreciation of relative size and girth, and that they are different things.

The leader wondered what other sort of sounds they could make, so K picked up a leaf, tapped it gently with his stick, and tilted his head the better to hear the sound. Other children tried this technique for themselves. W scraped a stick on a log, and the others followed suit. J wandered off to a branch, and shook it. Everyone went to listen, then wandered around base camp to see what other sounds could be made.

N took two sticks to batter either side of a tree trunk. J found a large stone, and hammered it on the ground, making a variety of sounds and movements. W whacked branches with his hand, so the leaves rustled furiously.

Some found a spot with lots of horizontal branches, which they shook, and used their sticks to scrape, tap, whirr and whisk the leaves. They enjoyed the contrast in sound made by the same beater on thin and thick branches and tree trunks.

Three children sat on a low branch and see-sawed, making the leaves vibrate noisily, and noticed the thud it made as it hit the ground under their weight. They riddled a stick between two branches, and called people over to listen, because the sound was quiet.

In today's sound-ridden world, it is not often that children have an opportunity to listen so carefully to such soft sounds, so it may take some effort to pay real attention to delicate and unusual sounds, which would normally have to compete with the ambient noises of their environment. That it is a pleasure to really make that effort is evident in the obvious glee of the children.

B picked up two large yellow leaves to flip against each other. An adult noticed, and exclaimed what a good sound it made, and asked if he could do it again. He obliged, then held up the leaves like earmuffs, and crunched them in his hands. She liked the sound so much, she had a go for herself. B was so proud – he had made such a good sound that a grown-up wanted to do it too. Wow!

Using different words to do with sound helps extend the children's vocabulary. They did not use many words that day, because they were busy making other sounds. But, if adults have come prepared with a list of potential 'sound' words, these can be dropped in to the activity as appropriate, such as this list of 'doing' words, or verbs:

● bang	● hammer	● scrape	● tap
● beat	● hit	● scratch	● thud
● belt	● jiggle	● scrunch	● thump
● blow	● knock	● shake	● thwack
● bump	● punch	● slap	● wallop
● clout	● rap	● smack	● whack
● crunch	● rattle	● smash	● whirr
● flip	● riddle	● strike	● whisk

At the end of the activity, these words could be introduced as the children talk about how they made different sounds, and back at school, they could be used as they describe to classmates what they did. The wider their vocabulary, the better they are able to express themselves accurately.

Children can also compare sounds they made with the sounds of conventional instruments: rainmakers, maracas and drums. During this session, they made their own instruments, and controlled sound like real musicians.

Especially with percussion, they learn how sounds are influenced by:

- the qualities of the materials used to make the instrument;
- the instrument's shape and size;
- the instrumentalist's movements;
- the instrument's movement.

Creative development is the main focus for this activity, but making music in this way involves other areas of learning too:

personal, social, emotional development: working together as a group, listening to each other, sharing a common enjoyable creative experience;

communication, language and literacy: finding words to describe actions and sounds, describing differences in sounds and materials used for instruments, listening carefully to instructions;

mathematical development: because the strong association with pattern and mathematics is also common to musical rhythm;

knowledge and understanding of the world: increasing awareness of the properties of materials, how sound travels and the cultural origins of music and musical instruments;

physical development: in the fine and gross motor skills used so carefully in making percussive sounds, and the gradual control which enables children to make the sounds they want to hear.

Fire!

Being out in the real open air with that most fascinating and perilous element, fire, is a special experience. For children, gathering twigs, making a fire from scratch and cooking on it, is magical. On this group's fifth visit, everything was prepared. The leader's bag contained some miraculously dry small twigs, newspaper, matches, a container of water and a packet of marshmallows.

Sweets!
L's big brother has been before, so he has heard all about this session.
I think we're going to light the fire!
Well, and if we do, where shall we put these marshmallows, do you think?
She got out a set of long, thin, sharpened sticks.
We'll eat them!
Yes, but we need to cook them. How shall we do that?
L stood up, and struggled to explain.
If you put them …
he pointed to the marshmallows …
on them … on sticks …
he pointed to the sticks …
and you put them on the fire and then you eat them!

He clapped his hands with excitement and pleasure at his own explanation. Everyone shared this pleasure, because L had never found this sort of thing easy. He was thrilled, because, as the leader confirmed, that was exactly what they were going to do. She took out some newspaper.

If I light this paper, will it burn for long enough to cook the marshmallows?
No.
Shaking heads showed that, although they were not quite sure, the intonation in the question meant that 'no' was the expected response; at a very early stage, children learn to detect when a question should have a 'yes' or a 'no' answer, and they usually try to please adults they respect.

So, what else might we need?

B got up, walked over to touch the sticks, and sat down again, scratching her head. This was a real puzzle.

Sticks, perhaps, L? But these ones with the point are for us to cook with, so what shall we do?

She looked around, questioningly. The children did not respond, so she took a few small twigs from her bag.

*Oh, **them** sticks!*

Yes, we need some small sticks to help the fire burn.

A stick was held across her palm as she looked around the group.

This stick is about as long as . . .

Your finger and up to your elbow!

Yes, just as long as that.

They would need a lot of twigs, just that size, to light the fire. They all rehearsed holding out their hands, to gauge the length from fingertip to elbow, which would be the measure for the sticks they would gather. After a further explanation, adults were confident that everyone understood what they had to get. L picked up a short stick from the ground, to measure against his hand.

That's a good length. What does it feel like?

Dirty.

Dirty wet, or dirty dry, do you think?

Dirty wet.

Will a wet stick burn in the fire, do you think?

In the fire . . . that's . . . no sun!

L raised his hands in slight confusion. Everyone else was confused too, but he was given time to work it out.

Does the fire need wet sticks or dry sticks?

Dry sticks!

If that's what L says, that's what we need. Dry sticks. How will we know if they're really dry?

The children did not know, and could not guess. They watched as she broke a dry stick in two.

Did you hear that? What sound did it make?

Bang!

Yes, a bang, but not a big bang: the drier the stick, the louder the bang.

They nodded sagely, because they were eager to go twig-hunting, for five twigs each, one for each finger on one hand, every one as long as your forearm and all as crackly as possible. This is quite a lot for young children to hold in their minds, and to achieve in the five minutes that have been allowed for the exercise. But time probably passes quite quickly when you are on such an important mission.

H looked on as the others gathered twigs. She was never keen to pick things up, possibly because of getting dirty.

She watched Y pick up a twig, measure and try to break it to length. He was rather anxious, wanting to get it right, and needed a little confidence boost. She listened as he explained to one of the adults.

It's crackly. It's dry. But it's too big. I broke it wrong!
Perhaps you could break it again?
Can I?
He did, and the adult asked H her opinion.
What do you think? Wet or dry?
H took the stick, measured it, and nodded.

She was encouraged to find more, but declined. Later, she seemed to be holding some twigs. She was reluctant to measure them, until an adult admired them. She handed them over; the adult made a neat little bundle, and gave them back. H smiled, proudly, put them across her hand to see how long they were, and continued to watch the others.

J was being helped to 'add on' by one of the adults. Adding on is a significant step in children's ability to manipulate numbers, because they no longer have to go back to 'one' each time they count. Realising that once they have *three*, the next one is *four*, is a mathematical milestone.

How many sticks have you got?
He handed her two.
One, two, so I've got two.
Two.
J passed her another.
Two, three.
Yes, I've got three.
Three, four.
He passed her the next one.
I've got four now. How many did we need?
Five!
J placed the fifth and final twig in her hand.

(Groups which have demonstrated greater understanding and counting skills may be asked to collect ten sticks: five small, from fingertip to wrist, and five larger, from fingertip to elbow. The complexity of the task depends on the ability of the group.)

While collecting, they had revised and developed their skills of counting, estimating, measuring, comparing, sorting and classifying; they had used their hand muscles to break the sticks, and listened, to work out how dry they were. They had all managed to find the right number of sticks of the right length. They returned to base camp, proudly put down their contributions, and counted: one, two, three, four, five. All exactly the right size – well done, everyone.

While they were away, the leader had organised the base camp for the fire. Leaf debris was cleared, and a concrete tile placed in the middle of the logs. Between that and the logs, she had placed some large sticks, making an inner ring. The children noticed.

What's that for?
They're bigger than our sticks.
But they're not logs, are they?
They weren't there before!

They were left to think it over, as the twigs were collected. One had a layer of greeny-blue fungus, which had not been noticed. This was put to one side, and wet wipes

were carefully used to make sure hands were really clean, in case they had inadvertently come into contact with the fungus. The sticks were counted in fives – not that the children know their five times table, but this was a model that there are easy ways to count large numbers.

Five, ten, fifteen –
But I didn't have five after the fungus was there!

Good mathematical perception, and now they had thirty-nine. That is enough to make the fire, so it was time to get on with the main business of the day.

They guessed the tile was for the fire, and the long sticks were to remind everyone to keep well back. There was a new way to move places on the logs; they rehearsed one by one, as they rhythmically chanted the words with the adults.

Stand, turn around, step back over the log. Walk around, step between the log and the sticks, and sit.

By then, the sequence was familiar. It was fun, but also vital for health and safety; they needed to know they could move if the smoke behaved unpredictably, and not, in a moment of impulse, be tempted to walk across the fire.

The newspaper was produced again, flat and folded. L remembered what his brother had told him. His usual low self-esteem was growing, because today he was making a major contribution to events.

You need to scrunch it up, scrunch it up!

He was handed a piece of paper, which he scrunched up, making a satisfying sound. Everyone else got some paper, and the scrunching created a new sound.

The paper was placed on the tile, and the children said that they must put small twigs on the paper, the ones they had collected, because small dry twigs burn easier than big ones.

Someone had once taught the leader that it was best to put the sticks in an upside-down V shape, so she arranged twigs like that on top of the paper.

It looks like a house! It looks like my house!
And mine – it looks like mine!

Sharpened sycamore sticks were given out. Children were shown how to hold them safely, resting on the ground with points in the air away from their faces, ready for the marshmallows. The sticks were special, made from sycamore, because other trees might not be safe to use as skewers. The children were shown how to spear marshmallows, pushing the point of the hard stick into the squidgy white stuff.

Everyone was ready for the fire-lighting. The matches came out of the bag, and a small voice started singing a song she had learned at home.

Matches, matches,
never touch.
They can hurt you
very much.

As everyone quietly joined in, the leader held up a small strip of paper, which fluttered in no particular direction. The day was calm, but usually there is enough breeze to indicate which way the wind is blowing, and therefore which way the smoke from the fire is likely to go. The children looked a little puzzled, so the point was not laboured, because it can be revisited another day.

Is it going to burnt up? Is it going to burnt up a bit?
Let's see.

The lit match was put to paper, and, much to everyone's relief, it burnt up a bit. The small flames danced around the paper, and caught the thirty-nine sticks alight. There was almost a meditative feeling; no-one spoke, no-one moved. Despite the calm, the smoke swirled around, so C needed to move. She changed position quietly and confidently, as they had rehearsed, but it did not help.

The smoke's following her!
It's moving around. It's following C!
It's coming all around!

Some more dry sticks persuaded the smoke to take a rest. The smell changed as the fire progressed from paper-burning, to twig-burning to big stick-burning.

The sounds changed too, as different materials caught light. Adults quietly commented; children responded by screwing up their noses to smell, tilting their heads to hear, and watching the colours, as the fire turned grey paper and brown twigs to yellow, red and orange flames, and then died back.

Will it be hot enough to cook marshmallows?
We can blow it! That will make it hotter.

After a good collective blow, and a few more sticks, the fire was ready for the food. Smells and colours changed along with the texture of the marshmallows; there was a soft hissing sound as their moisture escaped in the heat. Blowing made the fire hotter, but it made marshmallows cooler, as they were retrieved from the fire. They tasted smoky; they were hot and gooey, a darker, browner colour.

It's all gungy when it's been in the fire!
It tastes like fire!

Most adults will recognise how much scientific learning was in action here, as children observed the various effects of simple actions on a variety of materials. Not everything was articulated, because there is only so much information a child can make sense of in a short time. However, this first-hand experience would undoubtedly lay a firm foundation for scientific exploration in future.

The sticks were collected, hot chocolate was distributed, and quiet descended as they watched the fire die down.
It's going out.
The fire's going out now. It's finished.
Can we help it go out completely before we leave the woods?
Water. You have to have water.

Well, I have a large container here. Shall we pour it on?
Yes. It will make lots of smoke.
Will it make smoke or steam, I wonder?
No, it's steam. Water's wet, so it's steam.

Water was ceremoniously poured on the fire, which duly smouldered, faded and died, with steam taking the place of the smoke in the air.

The sounds came one after the other: a crack, a sizzle, as cold water hit the hot concrete tile. The smell changed too; the steam was not nearly as uncomfortable as the smoke. Each child's spontaneous comment spurred others to hear, see and smell the same things as their friends.

I can see the steam. I can see the steam from here.
And I can!

On the tile was now a pile of burnt, damp, black sticks. Were they cold enough to touch? Yes, they were cool now. They were like pencils, as was demonstrated on the tile. Everyone wanted a go, so they each took a burnt stick, now called charcoal, to make marks on a tree trunk.

C was entranced. Oblivious of everyone else, she assiduously scraped a pattern on the bark. Having gained confidence, she moved to a larger tree and worked on that, using bold, sweeping movements to make bold, sweeping marks.

Meanwhile, a couple of boys had spied some larger burnt logs, left by picnickers. They asked someone to come, because the logs were beyond the boundary trees. With effort, and adult encouragement, they lifted one, and brought it to base camp. They tested its mark-making potential on a tree.

It's the biggest pencil in the world!

They dropped that log, and went to find another. C had noticed them, and was standing alongside to watch, clutching her small stick from the fire.

She shyly indicated that she would like a go with the big log, so an adult helped her take the weight, and she manipulated the other end to make some marks, with a border around them. She finished, thanked the leader, and happily went back to her other tree.

Fire-making was an unforgettable experience for adults and children alike. Everyone was tired, with that satisfying weariness that comes from time well spent and a job well done, so the walk was slow back to the bus, with everyone clutching charcoal sticks to use for drawing later.

For such a potentially hazardous undertaking to be successful, as a learning experience and as a significant event in these children's lives, it has to be in a secure, stress-free atmosphere. This applies as much to the children getting the sticks of the right size and length as it does to learning how to be safe while sitting around the fire. There is challenge, but no pressure.

Throughout this activity, children needed the adults' support, for instance when the sticks were the wrong size, or the smoke was uncomfortable. But they were allowed space and time to get it right for themselves; the adults did not do it for them.

The joy of this session was shared by everyone, including the writer. A few weeks later, L, the child who had told everyone what was to happen in the account above, rushed across to greet the visitor to his classroom. Previously very withdrawn, lacking confidence and reluctant to initiate contact with adults, he grinned broadly and exclaimed excitedly:

I know you! We had marshmallows! We had a fire in the woods!

An analysis of the areas of learning covered in this activity is in Section Four.

Back at school: a note on resources

Reference has been made throughout this section to classroom-based activities which capitalise on the outdoor experience in the woods. Appropriate resources include reference books, photographs, story books set in woodland, plants, flowers and pieces of natural material such as bark, twigs, branches and creepers. A magnifying glass, or even a small microscope, can be used to examine closely or to make observational drawings. Creative and musical activities, which they have learned about in the woods, can be followed up with natural and more conventional resources in class.

Experienced practitioners will recognise the need to offer a full range of experiences which are open-ended and explorative. If there is a set of photographs taken during one or several sessions, children can decide how to sort or arrange them, in sequence, perhaps, or according to where in the woods they were taken, or who is in them. It is important that children have the chance to make choices according to their own criteria, rather then being set a task with a predetermined order or arrangement that they have to get 'right'.

KWL has made sets of high quality large photographs, some of which together depict a panoramic view of the base camp area, others tracing the blue string trail, and many of the same areas of woodland in different seasons and in different weather conditions. Children may not see the connections adults see, but they are nonetheless able to look at them, talk about them and sort them as they see fit.

Consider for instance these photographs of roots and branches, taken in the woods. Children are familiar with these particular roots and branches, so the quality of discussion promoted by these images outweighs any generated by more formal tasks, such as worksheets.

Any preparatory or follow-up classroom activities should follow the same principles as are applied in the woodland, that is: to encourage children to be confident and independent in their learning, to develop learning strategies and to use first-hand experience as the starting point for developing in all areas of learning.

The grown-ups

This section considers the duties of the project leader, and the role and training of other adults involved in the project, outlining the teaching and learning strategies employed, choosing a location, making a risk assessment, liaising with schools and organising transport. Children's families comment on how they think the project affects their children's development.

The project leader's role

Work with children and colleagues has already been described, but behind the scenes there is, as always, a significant administrative load, which includes liaison with schools, site risk assessments, training for adult colleagues, transport arrangements and the day-to-day resourcing of taught sessions. An ill-prepared project will certainly not make children's experience positive and productive, and may even fail to meet their needs.

A set procedure has been established when a new school joins the project. This ensures that necessary paperwork is completed and that everyone is fully aware of the requirements and processes, as well as the educational principles underpinning the project. There follows an account of the project leader's groundwork which enables the project to work successfully.

Letters are sent to schools, with a brochure outlining the project, and an offer to visit with photographic and other resources to inform the school of how the project functions. A follow-up phone call helps the project leader gauge the response, and usually she fixes a visit to explain further, and to outline the practical implications if the school is already keen to take part.

On this visit, the headteacher usually involves colleagues, and they discuss what happens, why it happens, and criteria for choosing the children. These vary from school to school, and the focus is usually on numbers, because everyone wants as many children as possible to go. An agreement is reached to go ahead, or to defer until later in the year; it is rarely the case that a school has dismissed the idea out of hand, and almost all local schools with early years pupils have taken part.

If everyone agrees to go ahead, arrangements need to be made for the appropriate number of adults to attend a training course over two days, at an indoor venue and in the woods. These people also need to provide evidence of a First Aid certificate and a Child Protection Criminal Records Bureau Clearance Statement.

The project leader checks that there is a suitable site available. Currently, this is at Tehidy, but there is on-going active research to find additional places, so more than ten groups (two a day) can be accommodated. If a different site is to be used, she will meet with the countryside ranger or an equivalent person to obtain permission to use the site, and outline the nature of the activities proposed. Dates are negotiated with the ranger.

Liaison with a bus company is the next step, including checking with the LEA that the company is on its list of approved transport, that vehicles are up to standard and that drivers have the appropriate clearances. Dates, pick-up and drop-off points and times are confirmed in writing.

Confirmation is now formalised with the school, including:

- the headteacher's signed agreement to take part;
- dates and times of visits;
- details of bus collection and return times;
- a risk assessment form (completed by the leader) to be signed by the headteacher.

Liaison with children's families is a priority. The leader always offers to meet the parents personally, although some schools prefer to keep this more informal. If so, they borrow resources and trained staff introduce the project to families. Parents/carers sign a consent form, and the school is asked to ensure that they have completed the appropriate County Insurance Form.

At this time, parents/carers are also asked for permission to use children's photographs in publications associated with KWL, which may be a school's newsletter, a project brochure or a report like this. Children's medical details are checked, including whether they have the recommended up-to-date tetanus vaccination (which also applies to the adults). Before the first visit, the leader contacts the school to double-check that there are no outstanding problems.

There is a set emergency procedure, provided by the local education authority, details of which are kept in the first aid kit in the leader's kitbag at all times, and of which the other adults have copies.

A larger bag contains cups, jug, whisk and flask of hot water for hot chocolate, biscuits, wet wipes and tissues, a towel, small plastic bags, paper towels, spare blue and orange tree ties, secateurs in case of a nasty bramble, the tarpaulin and rope. In addition, there are resources needed for planned activities, like plastic cups for 'smellpots', necessary items for the fire session and a basic but comprehensive reference book.

The need for checklists is obvious, because there is no corner shop in the woods to get anything that's been forgotten! Adults accompanying the children from school must bring with them:

- an attendance list with full names and addresses of children and adults
- parents'/carers' emergency contact numbers
- a copy of the permission slip to enable photographs to be taken and used
- a note of any children with allergies, known reactions to bites or stings or other medical conditions
- a full first aid kit and any authorised medication a child may need

Transport

The project's main expense is coach and driver hire. Suggestions that schools might use their own minibuses were considered, but this would incur the cost of a member of staff to do the driving, in addition to the required adult–pupil ratio, and extra administration for the leader, to liaise with a different driver from every school.

Another suggestion was that parents could ferry children to and from the woods, but there would need to be the standard Criminal Records Bureau checks on the drivers, and cars would need special insurances.

Ferrying eight or nine children needs at least two cars, with at least two adults in each car. A family problem might mean a volunteer driver was unavailable, and the school would need either to organise an alternative at the last minute or cancel the trip.

As far as the project is concerned, it was decided that having a coach company, with a professional driver who has all the necessary qualifications, clearances and insurance, and buses which must legally be maintained to a high standard, is worth the expense. Cutting transport costs is a false economy, because of all the administration required in ensuring everyone has directions, knows the best routes and can manage to arrive on time.

The project leader did extensive research into local bus firms, their costs and reliability. The firm used has contracts with many Local Authority schools and organisations, and complies with its rigorous requirements. On the whole, they are reliable, although occasional delays are inevitable. The drivers are child-friendly, understanding the need to park with the door away from the road, with room to disembark comfortably. The project leader regularly checks arrangements, and has built up an excellent relationship with the company, so this part of the organisation runs relatively smoothly.

Road safety would not seem to be a major element of a woodland learning project. The importance of children independently negotiating steps up and down has been mentioned elsewhere, and they are taught to look left and right as they disembark, and to listen out for cars. The parking place, on a small road leading to a few houses

and the golf club, in some ways requires more, not less, vigilance, because drivers may not expect to find children there.

The bus journey is part and parcel of the whole experience, and the time spent with adults and children together in the bus is an important aspect of developing the relationships in the group. It also gives children a sense of distance and place, and they see more from a minibus than from a car.

Choosing a location

In the introduction, the main reasons for choosing the Tehidy site are outlined. During training, all adults visit these woods, and complete a standard County risk assessment form, together with a member of the Cornwall Outdoor Education team. For the advanced leader course (described below), participants visit an unfamiliar site, which is rather more challenging, to assess whether it would be suitable for KWL use.

Apart from *health and safety* aspects, it is important to gauge the site's potential for purposeful and on-going *educational* activities. Some sites are perfect for a one-off afternoon visit, but there are many more requirements for a sustained programme of adventures and activities, so the exercise is both demanding and thorough.

The location must meet certain essential criteria, and should have additional desirable features. Any 'undesirable' features are considered in terms of whether or not they can be modified or avoided, and balanced against the site's overall potential, because nothing is perfect. A wonderful area which borders a sewage farm, or is too far from a drop-off point, has to be ruled out. Much depends on the children's ages and abilities, the distance from school, the variety of trees and plants, and access routes.

A risk assessment form completed by a member of the advanced leader course contained the following hazards and controls.

Hazards identified	*Existing controls*
condition of ground; slippery leaves	*reinforce moving carefully*
potholes and hidden roots	*check area; reinforce moving carefully*
fungi/berries	*reinforce rules: look but do not touch; adult supervision*
dog mess/litter	*remove/raise awareness*
bad weather – high winds or lightning	*check weather report – cancel visit*
children getting lost	*adult:child ratio high; play 1, 2, 3 to reinforce strategy*
fallen log on ground	*reinforce how to step over safely*
eye level twigs and branches	*cut back if sharp; demonstrate how to hold back*
damaged trees; broken branches	*advise warden to remove; avoid area if likely to fall*
strangers	*ensure adequate adult:child ratio; introduce adults in group by name so children know them*
snack: hot water in flask	*adult pours water; remind of not drinking until it's cool*
tarpaulin rope at adult head height	*ensure securely tied above head height*
position of bus door; traffic	*adult supervision; ask driver to park correctly*
incorrect use of seat belts	*check all secure before moving off*

It is worth noting that most safeguards are to do with raising awareness, not removing the hazard.

Assessing a site for woodland learning: a checklist

Educational criteria

ESSENTIAL

- suitably interesting, safe path for walking along;
- suitable space for base camp;
- wide range of trees: evergreen and deciduous;
- variety of leaf shapes and types;
- wide range of shrubs and ground cover;
- suitable conditions for fungi;
- some trees suitable and safe for climbing;
- owners/wardens sympathetic to the project;
- the right quality of light and shade to observe plant growth over periods of time;
- potential to erect tarpaulin when necessary.

DESIRABLE

- shallow water, small stream or pond, clean accessible, easily supervised;
- sufficiently quiet to hear woodland sounds, without too much ambient noise.

Health and safety criteria

ESSENTIAL

- woodland, with wardens or similar management;
- safe parking for drop-off/pick-up point;
- assembly point nearby to gather;
- suitable clearing within reach for base camp;
- base camp away from traffic noise;
- established path to get to base camp;
- fairly level path, negotiable in bad weather;
- not regularly used by dog-walkers, joggers etc.;
- relatively litter-free;
- sufficiently light but with some darker areas;
- no poisonous or dangerous plants or creatures;
- emergency contact (house, shop, pub) nearby.

DESIRABLE

- two exits in case of emergency.

The Toilet

What about the loo?' is a frequently asked question, which is not included in any of the criteria above, for good reason.

Problems are more anticipated than real: children are so involved, they rarely need the toilet. But since there is none in the woods, they weave a screen on their first visit, a little way from base camp. An adult from school must accompany them there, so they have some privacy but remain safe.

Walking the path: the leader's safety check

Before each session, the leader arrives to walk the path to base camp, noting potential hazards and, if necessary, dealing with them. A branch across the path, a leaf-filled hole, an overhanging dead bough, bramble creepers – these are examples of what an experienced, trained eye might note. What to do? Branches can be left on the path, a few leaves might be pushed aside to reveal the hole, the loose bough could be left, or knocked down if it is windy and it might fall. The bramble may be pulled to make it more obvious, or removed from the path.

The aim is not to remove all risk, but to ensure that everyone is aware of the hazards.

Sometimes, litter appears, such as discarded beer cans or wrappers. It can be left sometimes, so the children can discuss the issue and watch an adult (wearing gloves) carefully remove it to a plastic bag for later disposal. Litter is a major consideration in choosing a location, because an otherwise perfect spot may be unusable because of dog mess, glass or even syringes. Adults should not be subjected to such dangers on a regular basis, let alone young children.

During these early morning or lunchtime checks, the leader is usually alone, and able to absorb the atmosphere and sounds. Day by day, week by week, she becomes more familiar with the terrain: storing up information, noting what she might need to look up in her reference books, and enhancing her own professional practice.

Having consulted the local weather forecast before leaving home and looked for herself, she decides whether or not to put up the tarpaulin for shelter. It is held with sturdy nylon rope, at the right height – not so low as to garrotte an unwary adult.

While scrutinising the area to assess risks, the leader also notes the changes in the woodland. Fungi are a real source of delight, sometimes standing proud in the ground cover, often nestling in the roots or along the underside of branches. Using a stick, she might remove a few leaves to make it more obvious, so the children find it for themselves.

Colours change all the time: leaves get greener, browner, yellower, lighter or darker. Berries and spider webs appear, and, even in the autumn, there can be unexpected signs of new growth. In the spring, there are spectacular bluebells here, at first sprouting as if from nowhere, a rather hazy blue-green, and becoming a virtual carpet of blue in a short space of time.

In autumn, some, but not all, the leaves fall, covering what was bare soil, making the path crunchy before the

rain turns it to a comfortable softness underfoot. The sounds of footfall vary according to the season, the weather and the types of foliage bordering and overhanging the path.

These changes are one of the main reasons for taking the same group to the same place over a period of time. Only then can children appreciate how things grow and die, how colours come and go; and what is temporary, like bluebells, and what is permanent, like big trees.

On one or two visits, they can only see, hear and touch very little, but over several weeks, their knowledge and understanding build up, along with their confidence and self-esteem. This is also why records are so important, so the leader can ensure continuity and progression.

Being alone in a fairly isolated and unpopulated area, she needs personal safeguards, although nothing untoward has yet been reported in this area. She has a whistle and a fully charged mobile phone ready in her pocket, with the number of the nearest contact (the golf club) in its memory, along with her base number and the schools' numbers. Her colleagues always know where she is, so contact is easy if she needs to get in touch. Adults' health and safety must be considered in the risk assessment exercise, and foreseeable risks managed, as they are for the children.

There remains a problem for the leader: which of the talking points can be addressed in today's short session? Part of her skill lies in being able to match input with groups' abilities and interests.

Once basic administration is done (the project leader shouldering the main burden), it is in place for the series of visits, with weekly checks a matter of routine.

Training for other participating adults is both project-specific and generic, as detailed below. This directly benefits the adults, the schools and their pupils through:

- *heightened awareness of aspects of the curriculum;*
- *an enhanced understanding of how children learn;*
- *being able to observe a skilled practitioner in action;*
- *having additional experience of record-keeping;*
- *learning more about risk assessment procedures;*
- *taking responsibility for children's safety and learning;*
- *increased familiarity with curriculum documents;*
- *working closely with colleagues from other settings;*
- *sharing professional skills;*
- *working with other agencies and learning about them;*
- *personal professional development;*
- *increased self-esteem;*
- *confidence in their own abilities;*
- *being part of the project team;*
- *becoming more familiar with a beautiful local place;*
- *the enjoyment and fun of having such a good time with children and colleagues in the woodland.*

Who are the other adults?

A high adult–child ratio is needed for children to gain full benefit of this approach, which is very cost-effective long-term, because of the excellent start children have at this formative stage.

The local authority sets the minimum adult–child ratio for outdoor pursuits, which must be met by the school for the journeys, as the leader meets them at the woods. Groups are usually quite small, typically nine children and three adults from the school.

Recent exceptions have been made to accommodate larger groups, with the commensurate numbers of staff, and this is being closely monitored, to ensure there is no dilution of first principles, and that associated planning, learning and record-keeping standards are not compromised.

All adults who come to the weekly sessions attend training (see below). To ensure continuity, the same people should accompany the children every week, a time commitment of one half-day over several weeks. Ideological, educational, practical and financial considerations influence decisions about who should take part, with longer-term sustainability an important factor.

Teachers: Recently, some class teachers and one headteacher have made the weekly commitment, although this is still the exception rather than the rule. For headteachers, to commit this much time is unrealistic, especially if they already have teaching responsibilities. (In rural areas, there are many small schools, where heads teach for most of the week.) Releasing class teachers to go out with a small group has implications for supply cover expenses for most schools. Feedback to teaching staff is essential, and time is allowed for this back at school.

Classroom support staff: Teaching Assistants and Nursery Nurses tend to work with smaller groups, so timetables are more flexible. They have much expertise to bring to the project. They know the children well, and work closely with teachers; additional training is part of their professional development as they undertake more responsible roles in schools. They can also initiate and lead class-based activities based on woodland visits, set up displays and keep notes on children's progress and needs.

School governors: Governors are key to the success of any school initiative, in a prime position to gain and sustain the support of colleagues and fellow governors. Non-teaching governors may also be classroom support staff or regular volunteers in schools. Parent governors are well placed to explain and promote the values of the project to families of the children. Community governors bring many strengths into schools. Working with children (if they do not otherwise) gives them an insight into daily teaching and learning. Support offered by governors for the project has been an essential element in its sustainability and development.

Parents/carers: Family members are assets during most school activities; several parents were involved early on, and their contributions were invaluable. However, without them, children related better to each other as a group, and to other adults. Within the scope of the project, it would prove impractical to offer the training required for adults without some background in its pedagogical principles. Adults involved should, it was felt, be people who had a role with a responsibility to the school as a whole, rather than to one individual child, so it is a general rule that family members should not accompany their own children.

The decision was that at least one of the adults from the school should be a member of teaching or classroom support staff, and there should also preferably be a governor, who may or may not be an employee. This combination has worked well to date, and is likely to remain the pattern for the foreseeable future. Through the influence and support of all these key people, the project features in many schools' action plans locally, which augurs well for its future and for the benefits of future generations of children.

KWL training

Training is designed to enhance participants' existing skills in encouraging children to gain confidence: in working with others; in being independent but responsible; in trying out new experiences and ideas. Knowing our efforts will be rewarded builds confidence and self-esteem for adults as well as for children.

Trying out activities and challenges at their own level is vital, because adults can appreciate children's pleasure, satisfaction and potential concerns, all the more.

On each day of an intensive two-day course, they spend time indoors learning about organisation, risk assessment, health and safety regulations, relevant curriculum links and record-keeping. Then, they go to the woods to put theory into practical context. They play 'one, two, three, where are you?', learn to erect the tarpaulin, and hunt for materials to make a badger shelter, a log trail, a smellpot, an animal sculpture or an environmental decoration.

Theory is linked closely to practice, as the relevant curriculum documents are revisited in the light of the group's experience. One governor on a recent course confessed that at first she did not understand why training was needed to take children out for a few afternoons, but she was very pleased to have come back on day two, because it all fell into place. She realised it was about teaching and learning as well as health and safety. (She remains a regular and enthusiastic member of the team.)

Sometimes, health and safety can seem to be an overwhelming responsibility, but without appropriate safeguards in place the desired ethos cannot be established. Adults learn about risk assessment, and health and safety partly so they can pass this on to the children, who can then take on more personal and group responsibility, and be more independent.

Recently, an **Advanced Leaders Course** was piloted, to train current participants to lead groups from their own and other settings. Previously, only the project leader could do this, limiting the number of groups that could use the project. Once trained and formally assessed, advanced leaders can work independently in the woods, although general responsibility (for finances, planning, and overall supervision of both the project and the location) rests with the project leader. Course activities and tasks are specific to KWL, based on principles of good early years practice.

Everyone on the course has:

- completed a preliminary training course;
- achieved an appropriate first aid qualification;
- been checked by the Criminal Records Bureau;
- been recommended by their headteachers;
- accompanied children to KWL sessions with the project leader.

Applicants are asked to complete a short form, and to obtain a written reference from the school's headteacher and a personal referee. In planning the course, these elements were considered very important, as the advanced leaders, once trained and assessed, would undertake responsibility for groups from schools other than their own. This is very different from being with familiar colleagues; taking major responsibility for the health, safety and educational content of up to ten sessions with unfamiliar children and adults requires additional skills, so training is essential.

For some, the amount of administration and organisation undertaken by the project leader, and the attention to detail in curriculum planning, came as something of a surprise. However, thanks to checklists carefully prepared for them, and the balance between theoretical and linked practical elements, the feedback was very positive, despite the wet weather that accompanied the group to the woods, and the dangerously high winds that forced the cancellation of one session outdoors!

Courses are run by the project leader together with an early years specialist consultant. Members of Cornwall Outdoor Education contribute to health and safety, risk assessment and subject knowledge sessions. The Advanced Leader Course covers the following elements.

Curriculum links and subject knowledge: understanding how planning is linked with the statutory curriculum requirements, and appreciating how children learn through first-hand experience, active play, exploration and discovery, supported by adults.

Speaking, listening and questioning skills: analysing the language we use; how, when and if we should intervene; using observation and listening skills to assess children's current levels of understanding and confidence.

Planning and recording: knowing how to use, adapt and develop session plans to reflect personal strengths while ensuring that the special requirements of different groups are met; making basic assessments and records of children's progress; feeding back to school-based colleagues;

Advanced health and safety and risk assessment: raising awareness of issues and helping members feel confident in risk assessment and management.

Organisation and preparation: 'to do' lists, procedures for getting families' permission, booking coaches, liaising with colleagues, and other matters outlined above.

Practical leadership and management skills: identifying the range of skills we possess and need to take responsibility for KWL sessions; decision-making and problem-solving; leading a group of children and adults; valuing and acknowledging the contributions of all adults to the experience.

Assessment is through a course diary, and an observed session with children from another school. Course leaders look for:

- awareness of health and safety issues;
- good relationships with children and with other adults;
- good planning, organisation and preparation;
- effective leadership and management skills;
- speaking, listening and questioning skills;
- understanding of curriculum links and subject knowledge;
- ability to record significant features of children's behaviour and talk.

These comments are from participants following the assessed session with a group of children.

- *Making sure that every child felt valued and praising them for their thinking skills as well as their behaviour was not easy – especially as I am not very good with names.*
- *The most difficult objective for me was recording – on that morning the only thing I managed to write down was the names of the boundary trees.*
- *I have to admit that I enjoyed the session, despite being observed. However, the woods seem to have a calming effect on me as well as the children!*
- *I enjoyed the session in the woods. The children were very well behaved and interested in the environment. They joined in well and talked clearly to me and the other adults.*
- *The other adults were a big help, pointing out some things or repeating things I had said.*
- *I was concerned about the timing, but it worked out really well.*

How adults help children learn

Although all KWL participants are already skilled practitioners in their own fields, emphasis is placed during training on appropriate ways of interacting with young children, who gain self-esteem, confidence and maturity through positive personal experience. Some ways are better than others in encouraging them to think, reason and try out ideas for themselves.

The extent to which adults influence children's attitudes and learning styles cannot be over-stated. How adults approach problem-solving, especially if they 'think out loud' and acknowledge areas of difficulty, sets a pattern for children to adopt at their own level.

Children learn best if the adult working with them appreciates what they already understand, to build on that foundation by challenging them just enough, but not too much.

This is a much undervalued skill; judging how much a child understands can be tricky. Allowing time to observe, assess and evaluate a child's level of understanding is an important part of teaching and learning, not a luxury.

In the woodland sessions, there is a 'hands off' approach, with the emphasis on helping children gain independence: discussing *how* they can do something, or doing it *with* them, rather than *for* them.

Watching a video of the project leader at work, identifying and analysing the skills she uses, illustrates how an expert practitioner listens, and looks, evaluates a child's responses to a situation, and then decides how best to take the child forward through appropriate interactions and questions.

In due time, with suitable input, the child takes 'ownership' of the skill, concept or technique, and can manage alone. This independence is the aim, so children are secure in their understanding.

Strategies to encourage significant responses from children include:

- asking open-ended questions;
- asking 'I wonder ...' questions;
- making 'deliberate mistakes', both for the fun of it, and to model that we all get things wrong when trying things out;
- repeating, valuing and reinforcing children's descriptive, narrative and 'fun' language;
- regularly using 'grown-up' terms, such as 'I'm aware that ...', or 'We have a dilemma', so children can enjoy learning new phrases and vocabulary;
- acknowledging and praising achievement: 'good thinking', 'excellent listening', 'superb effort', 'well remembered';
- equally, giving praise for what they have learned;
- using positive language at all times, saving the command 'don't!' for emergencies.

In addition, *not* talking is a valuable and useful ploy, for instance:

- non-verbal cues: facial expression, body language, eye contact;
- modelling behaviour: if an adult stops to closely observe something, the action excites children's curiosity and leads them to do the same;
- offering a good role model at all times, like stepping over logs 'properly', listening carefully, sharing the fun;
- allowing children time to think before interrupting them – mentally counting to five is a good strategy;
- promoting silence as a good thing for thinking, reflecting and listening, by not interrupting at times when others are absorbed in their own thoughts.

All sessions were planned to meet curriculum requirements; course members have the planning sheets, specifying which areas of learning are addressed. Their experience and knowledge varies considerably, depending on how much they are involved in curriculum planning at school.

Record-keeping sometimes reminds us of the 'do I have to write about it now, Miss?' syndrome of our own childhoods, but it is an essential part of the teaching and learning process. Noting children's significant behaviours and remarks is helpful, both for the participating adults and for colleagues back at school. In particular, it helps reflect on how much has been achieved during the session.

Further information about curriculum planning and record-keeping is in Section Four.

Children's families

From the outset, children's families are informed about the processes, procedures and routines associated with the project. They have the opportunity to watch videos of previous sessions, and to discuss any concerns or issues with the adults involved.

They keep in touch through the work children do back in the classroom; through classroom displays; through talking with adults who go with the children. Most families know exactly what goes on because children talk about it all the time!

Most families have kindly completed a questionnaire, which asks them to comment on how much children talk at home about the project, and what sort of things they talk about. They are also asked what they think the child learned about. Asked if they think their child enjoyed it, the answer was a unanimous 'Yes – very much!' The following quotes are typical, so the families speak for themselves.

- *She learned all about the leaves, about different shades of green.*
- *He mentioned science in the wood, like duck, bird and tree etc.*
- *He learned about the countryside, trees, little creatures.*

- *It's a chance to get closer to nature than they may have experienced before.*
- *They learned to look at the woods from a different point of view.*
- *She enjoyed finding things, collecting stones and leaves, acorns and sticks.*

- *She was interested in new and dead leaves.*
- *He learned to respect the plants and animals of the forest.*
- *He mentioned different leaves. He didn't stop talking about the things they did there.*

- *He learned a greater awareness of nature. He told me about leaves, twigs and swans.*
- *She enjoyed making a leaf and mud mix and playing hide and seek.*
- *She especially enjoyed cooking marshmallows.*

- *Her confidence outside has been helped by the project, she worries less about getting herself (and others) dirty.*
- *He mentioned following the blue trail, having a camp fire, finding sticks, wood etc., and also said about relevant teachers present and what they did.*

- *She talked about the hide and seek song, the circle of logs, and that she was the leader.*
- *She also loved the bus ride and can remember the way still.*
- *It has helped her imagination and made her aware of places around her.*

- *He learned the safety of being in the woods and knowing how far he could go.*
- *She learned what to do if she got lost.*
- *It learns the child to work with others. The project is very good. It promotes independence.*

- *It was his first opportunity to go on a trip with others, to participate in activities and follow instructions.*
- *The project was well managed and supervised. I appreciated the minibus with seat belts and the hard work and efforts of all concerned.*
- *He learned how to do things on his own without me, and he learned how to be more confident.*

- *She learned to stay within a certain boundary, that water can be deep and trees are different.*

It is notable that there were no 'critical' or 'negative' comments, and that all parents/carers were able to identify particular advantages and learning developments specifically related to the visits.

The focus is on areas of learning which are traditionally linked with outdoor activities, stated in the aims of the pilot. However, few comments about mathematical and creative development are not an indication that these areas were not fully and formally addressed throughout. It is a signal that these aspects may usefully be highlighted in future discussions and meetings with families.

Families make sure that children are clothed appropriately for the visits to the woodland, and schools usually have a supply of boots or coats to borrow if necessary. In some cases, schools have supplied sets of waterproofs, funded by local businesses. These have been very welcome, but it does make them all look the same, and perhaps children are more comfortable and retain their individuality more in their own clothes. It is easier to keep track of a likely-to-wander individual if she or he is not dressed like everyone else. However, families are very grateful for the provision of appropriate outdoor clothing, and it helps schools, too, because there is less likelihood of the washing machine being needed when everyone gets back to base.

The curriculum in action

This section demonstrates how having fun in the woods meets curriculum requirements, outlining principles for planning along with examples of record-keeping.

Learning in the early years

This section is based on two key documents, because the first one informed the second, and both inspired the original pilot project. They are still major points of reference for current leaders at KWL. These documents are:

● *Quality in Diversity in Early Learning: a framework for early childhood practitioners*

A collaborative work by members of the Early Childhood Education Forum, published by the National Children's Bureau in 1998.

● *Curriculum Guidance for the Foundation Stage*

By the Qualifications and Curriculum Authority, published by DfEE in 2001.

These documents are quoted on pages 59–61 at some length, as a convenient reference, for readers to make the connections between them and the work described in the previous sections. For most, these connections will be already apparent, but there follows a series of examples, to demonstrate the planning process in action.

Throughout the accounts of practice and procedures, an analysis has been made of how the teaching and learning processes are evident in the adults' actions and words and the children's verbal and non-verbal responses. As stated, these magical moments in children's burgeoning understanding have been 'engineered', in the sense that they have been planned for.

Each of the activities planned, from getting ready to go on the coach, to getting back to school and following up the experience, are linked with **Foundations for Early Learning** and **Areas of Learning** in the above two publications respectively. The planning grid (page 70) enabled the team to ensure that every aspect was consciously covered, and adults could use it to help them focus their observations.

On occasion, this way of working highlights aspects of planning which are implicit, but perhaps not explicit. For instance, getting up and down the steps on the bus are everyday actions, which involve stretching, balancing, looking, holding, confidence and body awareness. Adults who appreciate how many skills are involved are less likely to hurry, or physically support them, but will help them learn to negotiate high steps on their own, and therefore to gain confidence in their own bodies. Children also learn to be patient with each other, although this is sometimes harder to achieve at this age. This apparently simple example is used to demonstrate that:

● children's gradual personal, physical and emotional independence is a priority;
● children can learn to be confident if adults empower them;
● children can learn dependence if adults fail to empower them;
● confidence in such an everyday action influences overall self-esteem, and this in turn affects children's disposition to try things out for themselves.

Quality in Diversity in Early Learning

This publication defined five (equally important) foundations for early learning.

Belonging and connecting: *from birth, young children are learning to form mutually respectful relationships with adults and other children in families, community and group settings. They are learning to make choices about aspects of their identities as girls and boys and as members of ethnic/racial, linguistic, social, cultural (and religious) groups.*

Being and becoming: *from birth, children are learning self-respect and feelings of self-worth and identity. They are learning to take care of themselves and to keep safe and well.*

Contributing and participating: *from birth, young children are learning to contribute and participate in families and other groups. They are learning to support each other, to care for each other, and to collaborate. They are learning to make choices and to understand how their choices affect others.*

Being active and expressing: *from birth, young children are mentally and physically active, learning to act on the world, to try things out, to see what happens. They are learning to express their ideas, thoughts and feelings, alone and with others, in a variety of ways.*

Thinking, imagining and understanding: *from birth, young children begin to think in a variety of ways: wondering, imagining, puzzling, dreaming, asking questions. They are learning to understand themselves and the world around them. They are learning to think critically and in a balanced way.*

Such analysis helps practitioners to ensure that they are considering every aspect of children's development when planning day-to-day activities. These foundations offered a framework for those planning the curriculum and devising the activities for the woodland learning project.

The illustration captures decision-making time when the children work out where to hide for 'one, two, three, where are you?' They are working out the best way to go, negotiating with each other and the adult, and using language and gestures to communicate with each other. They know the rules of the game, and operate within them, so they are in control. They want to be clever in hiding, but really want to be found! This small moment encapsulates aspects of all the above foundations, which would not be so if the adult just led them off to a convenient big tree!

Curriculum Guidance for the Foundation Stage

This important publication (influenced by principles outlined in *Quality in Diversity*) defined the six areas of learning referred to throughout this book.

In this passage, it argues that the Foundation Stage underpins all future learning by supporting, fostering, promoting and developing the following:

personal, social and emotional well-being: *in particular by supporting the transition to and between settings, promoting an inclusive ethos and providing opportunities for each child to become a valid member of that group and community so that a strong self-image and self-esteem are promoted;*

positive attitudes and dispositions towards their learning: *in particular an enthusiasm for knowledge and learning and a confidence in their ability to be successful learners;*

social skills: *in particular by providing opportunities that enable them to learn how to co-operate and work harmoniously alongside and with each other and to listen to each other;*

attention skills and persistence: *in particular the capacity to concentrate on their own play or on group tasks;*

language and communication: *with opportunities for all children to talk and communicate in a widening range of situations, to respond to adults and to each other, to practise and extend the range of vocabulary and communication skills they use and to listen carefully;*

reading and writing: *with opportunities for all children to explore, enjoy, learn about and use words and text in a broad range of contexts and to experience a rich variety of books;*

mathematics: *with opportunities for all children to develop their understanding of number, measurement, pattern, shape and space by providing a broad range of contexts in which they can explore, enjoy, learn, practise and talk about them;*

knowledge and understanding of the world: *with opportunities for all children to solve problems, make decisions, experiment, predict, plan and question in a variety of contexts, and to explore and find out about their environment and people and places that have significance in their lives;*

physical development: *with opportunities for all children to develop and practise their fine and gross motor skills and to increase their understanding of how their bodies work and what they need to do to be healthy and safe;*

creative development: *with opportunities for all children to explore and share their thoughts, ideas and feelings through a variety of art, design and technology, music, movement, dance and imaginative and role-play activities.*

The Foundation Stage Profile

To help children progress, practitioners need information about what the children know, understand and can do. Through observing children at work, and by making notes ... about what has been achieved, practitioners can make professional judgements about their children's achievements and decide on next steps in learning. They can also provide information for parents and carers about how children are progressing.

(Foreword)

To complete the profile, practitioners decide, with colleagues and carers, how well given statements describe the child. Personal, social and emotional development influences every aspect of children's learning, so relevant statements are quoted here for reference. (Readers unfamiliar with the FSP are strongly recommended to consult it for further information about its principles and practice.)

Personal, social and emotional development

Dispositions and attitudes

- Shows an interest in classroom activities through observation or participation.
- Dresses, undresses and manages own personal hygiene with adult support.
- Displays high levels of involvement in self-chosen activities.
- Continues to be interested, motivated and excited to learn.
- Is confident to try new activities, initiate ideas and speak in a familiar group.
- Maintains attention and concentrates.
- Sustains involvement and perseveres, particularly when trying to solve a problem or reach a satisfactory conclusion.

Social development

- Plays alongside others.
- Builds relationships through gesture and talk.
- Takes turns and shares with adult support.
- Works as part of a group or class, taking turns and sharing fairly.
- Forms good relationships with adults and peers.
- Understands that there need to be agreed values and codes of behaviour for groups of people, including adults and children, to work together harmoniously.
- Understands that people have different needs, views, cultures and beliefs that need to be treated with respect.
- Understands that s/he can expect others to treat her or his needs, views, cultures and beliefs with respect.
- Takes into account the ideas of others.

Emotional development

- Separates from main carer with support.
- Communicates freely about home and community.
- Expresses needs and feelings in appropriate ways.
- Responds to significant experiences, showing a range of feelings when appropriate.
- Has a developing awareness of own needs, views and feelings and is sensitive to the needs, views and feelings of others.
- Has a developing respect for own culture and beliefs and those of other people.
- Considers the consequences of words and actions for self and others.
- Understands what is right, what is wrong, and why.
- Displays a strong and positive sense of self-identity and is able to express a range of emotions fluently and appropriately.

Below, each area of learning in turn is considered in relation to the work described in this book.

Personal, social and emotional development

- disposition and attitudes
- self-confidence and self-esteem
- making relationships
- behaviour and self-control
- self-care
- sense of community

Without the necessary self-confidence and feeling of self-worth, most children find it hard to learn, because, just as success breeds success, so failure can breed failure. This may be true of a child who is very competent in some aspects of cognitive or physical development, but less confident and secure in others. The holistic nature of the project's work ensures that full weight is given to positively promoting personal, social and emotional development, because this is the context within which our pupils thrive.

The illustrations above demonstrate how children are encouraged to develop from working alongside each other to working together, because there is good reason to collaborate and co-operate. They find out that they can do things together, like moving a log (too big for one), or accommodating each other within the confined space of a tree. The pleasure of being part of the group is evident from the pride the girls have at first scaling the tree, then posing for their photograph, in a place that was inaccessible to them only a few weeks before.

Communication, language and literacy

- language for communication
- language for thinking
- linking sounds and letters
- reading
- writing
- handwriting

We are sitting down covering our eyes so we can't see where the people are going

Using reference books to find out about something interesting in the woods, hearing stories about woodland creatures; imagining what can be made for them (e.g. a shelter, or a piece of furniture); helping the leader write down names; making up names and remembering them by association; describing sequences of actions; finding words to describe colours; playing with sounds and syllables; speaking and listening to others; hypothesising, anticipating and predicting out loud; estimating; recalling events – these are all ways in which children explore language, and develop their communication skills.

Once back at school, there is something to talk about, to record in drawing and writing. Making a display helps to reflect on what has happened, like sequencing and making captions for drawings or photographs.

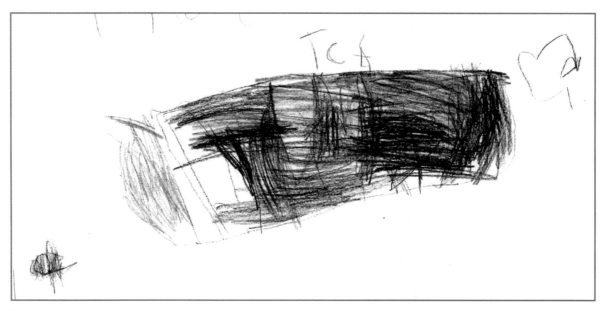

The crocodile tree, named by the children and drawn by one of them.

Notes made of children's comments when playing on the tree in the woods include:

- *This is where I jumped off to hurt my hand.*
- *Look at his teeth – he doesn't bite!*
- *It's the wind. That tree looks like it's falling over.*
- *It's special. I like climbing on it and I like feeding it with leaves. Actually, I'm feeding it now – I'm putting a leaf in his mouth.*

This imaginative language, typical of the storying children enjoy hearing and creating, is inspired by the surroundings and the encouragement to exercise their creative linguistic skills. Children who are reluctant to communicate in everyday situations find there is a reason, when they are inspired by something as exciting as a crocodile tree. An activity to make a house or shelter for a creature in the woods inspired the following comments:

- *That's a brilliant idea – we can work together!*
- *We could make a house for a dog.*
- *We could get rain in a bucket and put it in the bath.*
- *He eats slugs and snails and ferns.*
- *This is a step, and he goes through the door.*
- *He climbs up there to the top and then slides down.*
- *This is a bouncy thing for him.* (a pogo stick)
- *This branch is a good broom, I'll sweep the floor for him.*
- *I've got a duster.* (a branch with leaves)
- *This can be the shower.* (another branch with leaves)

Imaginative work such as this fosters creative development, design and technology based on using found items for a particular purpose, mathematical development in creating a structure to scale, physical development in the use of motor skills to achieve the desired product. Articulating ideas, working to a given brief, understanding and communicating between each other – these are all essential elements of the 'communication, language and literacy' area of learning, but like all good educational activity, there is consideration of the holistic development of the child. Each area of learning informs and is informed by each of the others.

Mathematical development

- numbers as labels and for counting
- calculating
- shape, space and measures

Mathematical awareness is both part of planning and a regular reason to stop and take further an action or statement such as described in the 'mathematical interlude' in Section Two. The illustration above is of a child playing hoop-la, a game children are familiar with at school. In the woods, they use available resources to make what they need to play, winding creepers around each other for hoops, finding the right length sticks for the poles and using pine cones or similar objects to keep a tally.

This game involves shapes, numbers, length, estimation for throwing and adding this time's score to the last one, which encourages counting on. Children help each other with techniques, because it is in everyone's interest for everyone else to succeed. Nonetheless, a winner is duly declared and praised.

Appropriate mathematical terms are used consciously by adults, so children gain an understanding of the lengths, weights, sizes, shapes and circumferences of different but similar items, from big logs to small leaves and twigs. Is this long enough? Is it too heavy? Do we need a third person to help us? Will it fit in there?

And, with experience, everyone knows how to estimate just how much powder and how much hot water are needed to make a good flask of hot chocolate!

Knowledge and understanding of the world

- exploration and investigation
- designing and making skills
- information and communication technology
- a sense of time
- a sense of place
- cultures and beliefs

I made a smelly pot

Exploring the environment develops children's sensory perceptions, as an aim, like walking the path, or as part of a task or activity.

For instance, when children look for objects to go into a 'smellpot', they indulge the joy of unpleasant smells as well as the more attractive ones.

Matching leaf skeletons to leaves still growing on trees (page 2), children learn about shapes, as well as the differences between 'dead', 'living' and 'once living' things, leaf identification, and classification.

There is no area of learning designated 'awe and wonder', but these illustrations, along with others in this book, show how an enjoyment of being able to explore in the woodland fosters a fascination and love of the natural world.

Me playing on the grass with bluebells

Physical development

- movement
- a sense of space
- health and bodily awareness
- using equipment
- using tools and materials

We tend to think of physical development in terms of gross motor movements, which children learn about as they make and use mud slides; help each other to balance and move on the rope swing; climb and move about in trees; learn to negotiate and avoid hazards on the path; learn to transfer their weight and the 'three point' principle (keeping two hands and one foot or vice versa in contact with the surface) of movement in challenging places like getting down from trees or up and down the bus steps.

However, of equal importance is the development of fine motor skills, the ability to handle precious things carefully, and to manipulate fragile materials with delicacy. Holding a marshmallow in the fire at just the right height, bearing in mind the plasticity of the stick and the effect of the weight on the end of it; making sure you do not interfere with others' sticks and marshmallows; being sure to balance your own body safely so you can concentrate on the smells, sights and sounds of the fire – these are all factors in managing to do for yourself what you want to achieve.

A balance of physical skills development is incorporated into the planning, to help children feel safe and in control, to know and respect their own limits, to understand the forces that apply when you are using your body in different ways, because there is no stress from lack of confidence. This confidence-building is part and parcel of leading children to independence, within their own levels of competence.

Creative development

- exploring media and materials
- music
- imagination
- responding to experiences and expressing and communicating ideas

A range of activities helps children develop their powers of perception and expression. Creativity is practised when children make items for imaginary or real creatures; decorate the woodland; try out different sounds using makeshift instruments, including their own voices, and experiment with sounds, words, names and descriptions. Science also involves creative thinking: making connections; recognising cause and effect; noticing patterns, similarities and differences.

Creativity is enhanced when children's perceptions are heightened: of colours, forms, shapes and spaces; 'natural' and made sounds. They learn about the qualities and potentials of available materials for making or organising. The senses are important creative tools, so sights, smells and sounds feature throughout: adults set the model by pausing to listen, scrutinise or smell what is around them, and drawing children's attention to how the senses inform and please or displease.

The process is as important as the product, but it is important to have a product, so time is allowed for the tasks to be 'finished'. Sharing and communicating with others about your own work is a vital part of the process: jointly negotiating the best solution, paying attention to what your friends think, and gaining hints from each other and the adults about how to achieve what you want.

Planning to meet children's needs across the curriculum

Mention is made above of the grid used in planning to ensure full and adequate coverage of the curriculum. Such a grid is reproduced below, for the activities described in detail in Section Two, with shaded areas indicating which areas of learning are addressed in each. Planners of the pilot project started with the curriculum, and devised an imaginative and progressive set of fun activities to meet it, rather then having a few 'bright ideas' and grafting them on to the curriculum.

Without a clear set of educational aims, decisions about which of the available avenues to pursue can be clouded and woolly. The grid therefore indicates with the symbol **X** those areas of learning (maximum four) which these particular activities address.

ACTIVITY	PSED	CLL	MD	KUW	PD	CD
The blue string trail	X	X		X	X	
Making base camp	X	X			X	
Naming the trees	X	X				X
Hide and seek	X	X	X		X	
Snack time	X	X	X	X		
Environmental art	X	X		X		X
Mathematical interlude	X	X	X			
Music-making	X	X		X		X
Fire	X	X	X	X		

It is notable that PSED and CLL are features of each of these activities, and of all the other besides, because these two elements of learning underpin all the others. Without a secure environment, opportunities to share ideas and concerns, question, explain, discuss and communicate, learning can be superficial and transitory.

It can be argued that each activity actually addresses each of the areas of learning, which is almost true, but planning focus ensures real engagement, and real opportunities for teaching and learning.

For these examples, creative development appears least on the grid, but of course a creative approach is implicit throughout. The overall programme ensures that this area of learning is given equal weight with others. Similarly, physical development is recognised in both strenuous activity and delicate movement and manipulation of tools and materials.

Planning cannot allow for the spontaneous, the immediate fascination with a found item or creature. But time can be used flexibly, which is in some ways equally important, for instance just to enjoy the feeling of cold rain on our skin.

On the following pages, two of the activities described in Section Two – naming the trees and making the fire – are analysed in the sort of detail which the planners considered when devising them.

Tree-naming

This apparently simple activity or ceremony presents the following opportunities for teaching and learning. Overleaf, those for the much more complex fire-making activity are summarised.

Personal, social and emotional development

- learning the importance of boundaries;
- being aware of their own and others' safety;
- sharing laughter and positive experiences;
- contributing to a group decision;
- helping each other to remember the names;
- listening to each others' ideas, and evaluating them;
- encouraging each other to contribute to the discussion;
- knowing that what they say will be taken seriously.

Communication, language and literacy

- using appropriate language to describe the trees;
- listening to and evaluating others' ideas;
- adding new words to their active vocabulary;
- practising and remembering the sounds of the names;
- giving and following directional instructions;
- recalling, sequencing and recounting the experience later.

Mathematical development

- using mathematical descriptors (tall, long, sideways);
- using directional words (over there, behind, in front of);
- noting overall and detailed shapes;
- comparing relative scale (bigger, smaller, higher, lower);
- estimating (how high, how tall, how long).

Knowledge and understanding of the world

- appreciating similarities and differences in the four trees;
- observing features of the trees;
- noting what is part of the tree and what is growing on it;
- learning names such as bark, twig, branch, leaf, root.

Physical development

- using different types of movement between the trees;
- learning to climb and swing safely from appropriate branches;
- stretching and crouching to examine the trees;
- gaining confidence through familiarity with the terrain;
- exploring about their own capabilities and limitations.

Creative development

- listening to the different sounds in and around the tree;
- using language creatively to make the tree names;
- comparing and contrasting colours, patterns, shapes, textures in and on the trees;
- actively using all their senses (except taste);
- using experience for creative work back at school.

Fire!

Personal, social and emotional development

- paying attention to the rules; rehearsing movements;
- awareness of the boundaries of behaviour;
- working as a group to get sticks for the fire;
- learning how to be safe, to manage potential fear of fire;
- sharing a significant experience, expressing feelings;
- taking responsibility for finding sticks, scrunching paper.

Communication, language and literacy

- use of descriptive language: similes, adjectives;
- use of positional language: higher, lower, over, under, on;
- predicting what will happen if . . . ;
- listening and responding to each other.

Mathematical development

- measuring sticks; breaking longer sticks to length;
- counting up to 5, then in 5s – how many altogether?
- classification of long and short sticks;
- sequence of cups – predicting which colour will be mine?
- comparing and estimating length of sticks.

Knowledge and understanding of the world

- fire produces heat; the temperature varies;
- changes in paper from flat to scrunched up to burning to burnt to smouldering;
- sticks blazing, turning black in fire, then becoming charcoal, which can make marks;
- awareness of wind direction, and its effects on smoke;
- difference between smoke and steam;
- water extinguishes fire and causes steam to rise;
- blowing drink makes it cold; blowing fire makes it burn;
- dry sticks burn; wet ones do not;
- dry sticks crack when bent; wet sticks do not;
- animals will perish so take care when lighting fire;
- marshmallows change colour, texture, form, smell, taste.

Physical development

- balance when moving around on the logs;
- following a sequence to move around logs safely;
- fine motor skills to snap sticks to right length;
- balancing cooking sticks safely at right height.

Creative development

- smells: wood, paper, marshmallows, doused fire;
- sounds: paper scrunching, sticks burning, hiss of steam;
- sights: colours in flames and light they cast;
- tastes: food: linking smell to taste;
- touch: wet and dry sticks, feeling of heat from fire; texture of marshmallow on sticks;
- use of imaginative, expressive language.

Assessment and record-keeping

Formative records

The leader and other adults keep records of what children have said and done, and how these reflect children's development in one or more of the areas of learning outlined above. Set activities are planned according to these areas, so there is a focus and a framework, a checklist to ensure that each area is considered.

Throughout this book, analysis has been made of how observation of children's actions, and listening to their comments, informs practitioners of their learning and learning needs. Any system to record observations must be easy to use, enabling adults to record significant observations, and to use these records to develop their own skills, through recall of and reflection on the session.

During training for advanced leaders, course members view a video of children at work, for which they have a transcript. In pairs, they share ideas about the evidence they gather about children's learning, to note on the transcript. It will not surprise readers to learn that they are already very aware of what is going on, but such an exercise helps us all to hone our own skills; comparing notes with a colleague helps us to be more perceptive and analytical than we might be on our own.

A simple proforma helps adults to make notes for the class teacher and other adults. Notes can be made on the spot, but this should not isolate the adult from the on-going activities; it is best to make time immediately they get back to school. The example below illustrates how an experienced practitioner can recognise the mathematical, physical and social significance of comments and actions during the stick-collecting activity prior to building and lighting the fire. Children's words are underlined.

Date 06.03.03	week 6	School: Camborne Nursery School
ACTIVITY	Collecting sticks for lighting the fire	
NAME	COMMENT OR ACTION OBSERVED	AREA OF LEARNING
Kielly	found 5 sticks - I've got enough now 1 2 3 4 5: counts to 5, first time she has managed to count one-to-one - getting confident in counting accurately	PSED MD
Maria	found 8 short sticks - I'll have to throw some away - subtraction - counted, threw away 2, then counted and threw away one - 5 left in her hand - Look!!	MD
Naomi	shared her sticks with Billy - you can have some of mine Billy, I've got too many and you've only got 3 - sharing (not usual) - very long statement for her.	MD CLL PSED
Jordan	very insecure at first, watched others and then copied them. S helped him count. I've done it, I've got 5 short sticks . Now I have to find five long ones!	MD PSED
Beth	that's green fungus - we can't have that one cos Sandie said we mustn't touch the fungus - remembered info from last week, shared with J.	PSED KUW
Billy	long stick, measured against others, broke it carefully to size - good fine motor movement - listen! It made that crack sound Sandie made!	PD CD MD
Jo	that one looks long enough for my arm - estimating length - measured it against his arm - that will do - just right! I don't have to break mine, do I?	CLL MD

Me hiding with Keeran

These records, made by the project leader about children in one group, are about general attitudes and dispositions, a vital element in creating an ethos appropriate for young children's learning. Most readers will recognise how typical are the children described of this age group.

A: A born leader, he had us organised from the first session; therefore difficulty learning that you don't always have to be leader and talk all the time. Began to realise you can shine within a group. Listening skills still need working on.

B: Began quite withdrawn and not very enthusiastic ('Is it home time yet?'); later asked a lot more questions; loved the fire; able to take risks climbing trees.

C: Full of energy, keen and confident. Some bad days, a bit weepy, but responsibility of leading group on trail refocused him. Wood environment allows different approaches to children's needs.

D: Not comfortable initially, chewing clothes, but listened well and took part willingly; now a lot more adventurous, taking risks and climbing.

E: Very comfortable in the woods, listened and carried out activities, observing and asking us to look; overexcited if asked to do something in front of a group, but confident enough to have a go.

F: Co-operative, observant, aware of her environment, very detailed observations. Can tend to overpower, so group problem-solving work is good to encourage her to interact with others.

I saw a bird

G: Going off by herself, not listening, not aware of base camp rules, a loner; could tell what orange tape was for but didn't heed it. Tries to initiate relationships by asking questions, but does not respond to children's replies.

H: Withdrawn, not happy to be part of a group, but loved snack time – opportunity to interact with group, handing out biscuits, responsibility gave confidence.

I: comfortable working by himself, but got better working in groups, making suggestions, helping others.

Summative records

These practitioners' comments note significant behaviour shifts for each child.

I like that tree and I like
Sandie and I like you

Personal, social and emotional development

- She was very isolated, but she now has many friends and other children talk to her much more; she is now part of a group.
- She would often isolate herself from the other children and particularly enjoyed relationships with adults. In the woods, she learned to play with others and enjoy their company.
- She lacked confidence to try things out, but her family took her to the woods and she was able to show the way.
- He was the only child who was unable to stay within the four physical boundaries, but on the very last session he coped successfully.
- He had previously seemed more agitated. He is now more relaxed.
- He is showing his sense of humour!

Communication, language and literacy

- Expressive language has developed and a wider vocabulary is evident.
- His skills of communication and interaction greatly improved.
- Her language has improved and much of her frustration has gone. She has shown that she can communicate and tell you things.
- She is much more confident in her writing. She previously had said, 'I can't spell'.
- She started 'writing' when she brought the charcoal sticks back from the fire in the woods.
- He found books about woodland creatures and shared them with his friends.

Mathematical development

- She began to count on after she managed to do it with her leaves in the woods.
- He began to sort things in the sand tray and in the nursery garden, which he had not done before. He looked for things that matched each other.
- She is much more confident about estimating or guessing now; not so worried about getting things wrong.
- He tries to tell the time when the bus is coming, and can manage nine o'clock and half past nine.

Knowledge and understanding of the world

- He now asks questions and wants to know why and how things work.
- On the last session she initiated a trail-making activity.
- He is now particularly able to look and observe things closely.
- In the nursery garden he now looks under logs to find slugs and minibeasts.
- He has a good sense of direction, and can describe the route to the woods and back.
- She is interested in why plants die, and looks after classroom plants to keep them alive.
- He has tried to find pictures of badgers and hedgehogs in storybooks and information books.

Physical development

- He proved to be very able physically and was extremely confident when running and climbing.
- The freedom of the outdoors made a huge difference.
- Her gross motor skills developed a great deal.
- He was able to take risks, particularly in the area of physical development.
- She is now prepared to get dirty, run and climb.

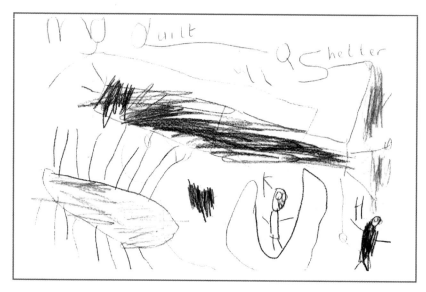

My quilt shelter

Creative development

- Her drawings are more confident; she puts everything in to explain things to people who didn't go.
- She understands colours now, and sorted the leaves brought back from the woods into different coloured sets.
- He has become more confident in handling art materials – getting his hands dirty in the woods has helped him concentrate on what he is making, rather than worrying about dirty hands.
- He got other children to copy the sounds he made, and asked them to pretend they were using a real tree, not a drum.

Such assessments are supported with ample evidence, such as weekly notes, copies of children's drawings, writing, and photographs taken at school and in the woods. With appropriate related resources and activities back in class, children can look up what they want to know, experiment with colours and shapes, and use photographs to sequence and recall the time away from the classroom. Such resources help children to recall, reflect and demonstrate how much they have done, how much they have learned, and how much they remember.

Conclusions

This section summarises the main issues, and considers the project's potential sustainability and expansion.

Principles of Kernow Woodland Learning

In the introduction to this book, the principles of the woodland learning project are outlined, and here is a summary of the main points which influenced the work from the outset.

- The woodland is the focus, the starting point and the primary resource base for all activities.
- Children have freedom to explore within clearly defined boundaries.
- There is an appropriate, well-rehearsed code of behaviour and ample opportunity to follow up observations and comments.
- All aspects of the early years curriculum are addressed; there are no 'paper and pencil' exercises, but experiences have a direct impact on children's progress in all areas of learning.
- Sessions are cancelled only if there is a health and safety risk, such as high winds or deep snow, following the adage: there is no bad weather, only inappropriate clothing.
- Each session is carefully planned, and thorough records are kept, with close reference to the appropriate curriculum documents.
- KWL is for all children, with potential to extend the more able and to support those with particular needs.
- All adults involved are trained in first aid, health and safety, risk assessment, organisation and curriculum issues relevant to the setting and the age of the children.

That these principles are of value to children and adults has been demonstrated in the account of the project's work, and illustrated by the comments of children involved, their families and the adults who work with them. In every sense, they comply with the **Principles for early years education,** *outlined in the Foundation Stage Curriculum Guidance, which is equally applicable to all early years education for most children. These are quoted below, so readers can make appropriate connections with the examples and information in the other sections of this book.*

Principles for early years education

The Foundation Stage Curriculum Guidance states that, to be effective, an early years curriculum should be carefully structured. In that structure, there should be three strands:

- provision for the different starting points from which children develop their learning, building on what they can already do;
- relevant and appropriate content that matches the different levels of young children's needs;
- planned and purposeful activity that provides opportunities for teaching and learning, both indoors and outdoors.

Effective education requires both a relevant curriculum and practitioners who understand and are able to implement the curriculum requirements.

There should be opportunities for children to engage in activities planned by adults and also those that they initiate themselves.
Children do not make a distinction between 'play' and 'work' and neither should practitioners. Children need time to become engrossed, work in depth and complete activities.

Practitioners must be able to observe and respond appropriately to children.
This should be informed by knowledge of how children develop and learn and a clear understanding of possible next steps in their development and learning. Early years experience should build on what children already know and can do. Practitioners should ensure that all children feel included, secure and valued. Above all, effective learning and development for young children requires high quality care and education by practitioners.

Well-planned, purposeful activity and appropriate intervention by practitioners will engage children in the learning process and help them make progress in their learning.
For children to have rich and stimulating experiences, the learning environment should be well planned and well organised. It provides the structure for teaching within which children explore, experiment, plan and make decisions for themselves, enabling them to learn, develop and progress.

Descriptions of activities in this book have emphasised the quality of planning, the richness and variety of the stimulating experiences offered. Equally, emphasis on skilled observation, careful listening and appropriate intervention underlines the worth of skilled, trained practitioners. If this education is appropriate and valuable for this group of schools in this particular area, it is certainly able to benefit children elsewhere, throughout their early years education and beyond.

Sustainability of the project

Over the last year, the project has expanded to include more schools, to train more adults to accompany children to the sessions, and to train more advanced leaders to organise and run sessions with schools other than their own.

Those currently involved all work with the Foundation Stage, although it is clearly equally appropriate for children at Key Stage 1 and beyond. Work is in progress to ensure that KS1 subject areas are matched with learning activities outdoors.

Ideally, this sustained experience should be available twice a year for each year of a child's early years education to enable them to build on previous experience, to tackle more ambitious tasks and activities according to their abilities.

There are clear staffing and funding implications for the future of the current project, and even more if it is to include older children.

Local preschools are very interested in using the project, but financial considerations put it beyond the means of small independent playgroups. Current funding by the Camborne Pool Redruth Success Zone promises to continue into the new Excellence Cluster which will succeed it. Other implications are to do with finding appropriate locations and training more staff.

Headteachers whose schools have been involved are unanimous in their praise for the project, and fully supportive of its expansion. Clearly, they are key professionals, who will join KWL personnel to discuss, with appropriate members of the local education authority, ways to enable more children to have this excellent experience in their early years of education and life.

In conclusion, it can be firmly stated, on the basis of evidence offered in this book, that here is an educational venture second to none. In the considered opinion of the writer, who has spent over thirty years in primary education, investment in this project is an investment in the future of the children who benefit from it. It meets the principles and standards demanded by the statutory curriculum documents, but, more importantly, *most* importantly, it meets the needs of the children.

Index

It is part of our literacy work with children of all ages that we model how to 'look things up' – in catalogues, reference books or telephone directories – and to encourage them to do the same.